The O
of Home

First published by O Books, 2010
O Books is an imprint of John Hunt Publishing Ltd., The Bothy, Deershot Lodge, Park Lane, Ropley,
Hants, SO24 0BE, UK
office1@o-books.net
www.o-books.net

Distribution in:	South Africa
	Stephan Phillips (pty) Ltd
UK and Europe	Email: orders@stephanphillips.com
Orca Book Services	Tel: 27 21 4489839 Telefax: 27 21 4479879
orders@orcabookservices.co.uk	
Tel: 01202 665432 Fax: 01202 666219	Text copyright Jennifer Kavanagh 2010
Int. code (44)	
	Design: Stuart Davies
USA and Canada	
NBN	ISBN: 978 1 84694 264 8
custserv@nbnbooks.com	
Tel: 1 800 462 6420 Fax: 1 800 338 4550	All rights reserved. Except for brief quotations
	in critical articles or reviews, no part of this
Australia and New Zealand	book may be reproduced in any manner without
Brumby Books	prior written permission from the publishers.
sales@brumbybooks.com.au	
Tel: 61 3 9761 5535 Fax: 61 3 9761 7095	The rights of Jennifer Kavanagh as author have
	been asserted in accordance with the
Far East (offices in Singapore, Thailand,	Copyright, Designs and Patents Act 1988.
Hong Kong, Taiwan)	
Pansing Distribution Pte Ltd	
kemal@pansing.com	A CIP catalogue record for this book is available
Tel: 65 6319 9939 Fax: 65 6462 5761	from the British Library.

Printed by Digital Book Print

O Books operates a distinctive and ethical publishing philosophy in
all areas of its business, from its global network of authors to
production and worldwide distribution.

The O
of Home

Jennifer Kavanagh

BOOKS

Winchester, UK
Washington, USA

There was a time when travelling throughout the world that I felt acute loneliness. I could hardly wait to return to familiar territory. Gradually that feeling diminished and vanished completely after I had spent almost five years in captivity. During my four years of solitary confinement I had to come to terms with my inner life in a new way. Today, I feel at home in virtually any part of the world for I carry 'home' within. There is a great deal of truth in the statement that homelessness is a state of mind although that is not the whole truth of course. It is utterly miserable, and frightening to be without shelter and vulnerable to the world. As Jennifer Kavanagh points out in this book the concept of home means so much more than having an adequate place to live. It is, as she says, 'Where we all want to be'. This book is important reading for anyone who would seek to explore the concept further. It would form an ideal basis for discussion groups or those who are seeking to establish support for the homeless. It does not pretend to contain all the answers but it certainly stimulates thought around a subject which so many of us take for granted.

Terry Waite CBE

Home - in the heart, in the head, a physical space that shifts and moves with emotions, a locale, a dream, a site of conflict and cruelty and also intimacy and safety, homelands, exile - all this and more are explored in this tender and moving book which makes you wonder what home really is or ever was.

Yasmin Alibhai-Brown, Columnist and author of
Settler's Cookbook a memoir

This is a book that opens the heart. Tender, thought-provoking, compassionate, and insightful, it leads us on a circular journey from understanding what we need and mean by home, through experiences of homelessness and forced displacement, to a true coming home to the self and the divine.

Marian McNaughton, Chair of Trustees of the
Joseph Rowntree Charitable Trust

Home - the longing for it, the loss of it, the need for it - is one of the defining images in a modern world of travel, globalisation and uncertainty. In exploring the many meanings and interpretations of the word, Jennifer Kavanagh has produced a memorable and important book.

Caroline Moorehead, author of *Human Cargo*

If 'home' is a theatre of soul, then that which is front-stage in one life, may simply be waiting back-stage or in the wings of another. Jennifer Kavanagh is a good narrator, she takes us to the heart of what matters in so many lives, and I am at home in the audience, listening with so many others, and saying to myself: Oh Yes! Oh Yes! This is the way it is, and, surely together in some way we can help each other to feel more at home in the world.

Lindsay Halton, Architect and author of *The Secret of Home*

CONTENTS

.

For my family

In the beginning is relation
Martin Buber

This book comes from my own experience and that of the dozens of people I have asked without warning or preparation: "What is home to you?" To all who gave of themselves with such honesty and depth, thank you. Many names have been changed.

All references in the text refer to the editions of books listed in Further Reading. Where there is more than one book by an author, the date of the publication is given.

1

The O of home

Introduction

When I began to write this book, the credit crunch was a mere gleam in the eye of a malevolent gnome.

A period of financial crisis, when much that we have held certain has been turned upside down, is a better time than most to challenge ingrained assumptions: not least in the context of "home". Our preoccupation with privacy and security; community as an exclusive group of like-minded individuals; the inviolability of borders and nationhood; the superiority of the human race. The notion that some groups of people are somehow different, lesser, "other". Or that home is synonymous with four walls, investment, status and identity.

We have the opportunity not only to look squarely at how things are, but also to dare to dream of how they might be.

In looking at the subject of home, we need to explore not just what it means for us as individuals, but also in the context of our communities, of our nations, and of our species. We need to consider not only what our outer houses mean, but those within.

The shape of this book is circular. We begin with our material home: bricks and mortar as shelter, all the accretions that Western society has added – and what it means to live without one. We then move outwards to consider home as relationship: with family, neighbourhood, local community, and what it looks like at different times of our lives. The circle widens to include home as identity, nationality, belonging to our country; and looks at migration, both voluntary and enforced. The possibility of relationship in humanity, community without borders. "The sacred home" of us all is the earth, together with other created beings. We consider our place on the planet and our responsibility to other life-forms. We then turn full circle to consider the only true home: we will never be "at home" in any place, unless we are at home to ourselves, comfortable in our own skins. Coming home to self, and how we might achieve it; the spiritual dimension for those of faith.

The circle (O) is itself an ancient symbol, central to many traditions of the world, and represents many of the qualities of "home". As a closed shape it is all embracing, associated with protection, providing safety for all within. Carl Jung considered its protective, nurturing quality to be part of the mother archetype. With no part greater than another, it also represents democracy and is the preferred shape for an assembly of equals. With no beginning or end, the circle represents eternity. For Native Americans, the shape of the circle represents the circle of life itself. According to Black Elk, a holy man of the Oglala Lakota Sioux:

Everything the Power of the World does is done in a circle. The sky is round, and I have heard that the Earth is round like a ball, and so are the stars. The wind in its greatest powers whirls. Birds make their nests in circles, for theirs is the same religion as ours. The sun comes forth and goes down again in a circle. The moon does the same, and both are round. Even the seasons form a great circle in their changing, and always come back again to where they were. The life of man is a circle from childhood to childhood, and so it is in everything where power moves.

The circle represents oneness and unity, completeness and wholeness, all of the parts of our being: the cosmos, the cycle of seasons, and of our lives on earth. Time, tides, and breath.

In each section we will include the "broken circles": those who are without home, whether a shelter, a nurturing environment, a country of the heart, or a sense of home in themselves. We will also consider the unconsidered other residents of our planet.

Home is a central and emotionally laden concept. Sometimes it is a present reality. Sometimes it is a yearning for a childhood experience, real or idealised; sometimes it is a dream of something that has never been. In children's games it is the place of safety where nothing can touch you; on a computer, it is the personalised place to which you can return. In dream interpretation, a house is often seen as a symbol of the self, and is a key to how we regard ourselves.

Home is where we all want to be.

2

The O of protection

Bricks and mortar

*As for a Shelter, I will not deny that this is now a necessity of life,
though there are instances of men having done without it for long
periods in colder countries than this... But probably man did not live
long upon the earth without discovering the convenience which there is
in a house... We may imagine a time when, in the infancy of the human
race, some enterprising mortal crept into a hollow in a rock for shelter...
From the cave we have advanced to roofs of palm leaves, of bark and
boughs, of linen woven and stretched, of grass and straw, of boards and
shingles, of stone and tiles. At last we know not what it is to live in the
open air, and our lives are domestic in more senses than we think.*
Thoreau, 17

In the spring of 1845 Henry Thoreau built with his own hands a
cabin in the woods and on the shore of Walden Pond, outside
Concord, Massachusetts, USA. He lived there alone, a mile from
any neighbour, and earned his living by the labour of his hands.
He wrote:

I have thus a tight shingled and plastered house, ten feet wide
and fifteen long, and eight-feet posts, with a garret and a
closet, a large window on each side, two trap doors, one door
at the end, and a crick fireplace opposite...
    I went to the woods because I wished to live deliberately to
front only the essential facts of life, and see if I could not learn
what it had to teach, and not, when I came to die, discover that
I had not lived. I wanted to live deep and suck out all the
marrow of life, to live so sturdily and Spartan-like as to put to

rout all that was not life... to drive life into a corner, and reduce it to its lowest terms (*ibid.*, 31, 59).

Anton and Gwyneth have created a way of life that Thoreau would have recognised. In the woods in hills in Eastern Cape, South Africa, they have built a wooden house and several cabins, a pottery for Anton, and for Gwyneth, a singer who runs an opera company: a little opera house. They have done the work themselves: a pottery wood-burning stove, the plumbing, the long-drop lavatories. Students come to learn singing or pottery; goods are for sale. There are fruit trees, vegetables and herbs: it's a self-sufficient lifestyle with inhabitants deeply involved in the local black and white community.

Human beings have always sought shelter – from inclement weather, wild animals and from hostile human beings. In the twenty-first century, shelter ranges from something not that different from what our ancestors knew to housing on a scale they would have found unimaginable.

As a small child I remember feeling that houses were only for shelter, that it was much more natural to be outside, in the open air. Much to the consternation of my mother, I escaped from the house whenever I could.

Four-year-old Titus, when asked about home recently, spoke more of his garden. Only when he was tired did he want to go inside. Three-year-old Jamie, when asked about home said, "Walls". Basic.

Built for shelter, houses have taken on an extraordinary array of properties and roles.

Let us look at what home is not.

The word has been so abused, so muddled, that we have almost been persuaded that home is synonymous with a house. Magazines such as *Ideal Home, Homes and Gardens, Real Home*; advertisers – "Home Broadband for a Happy Home" – estate agents and furniture salesmen, try to imbue bricks and mortar with all the qualities of warmth, security, love and familiarity that we associate with "home".

The blurring of the distinction is not helpful. When used accurately, the subtlety of difference is important. "Home-made", "home-baked" have connotations of wholesomeness, a whiff of family nurture; "house-proud" is only about cleanliness, care for the material condition of a building. And "house-bound" – no one would substitute the word "home" for a state of feeling imprisoned.

Nor is home just an address.

"Where do you live?" is a mainstay of introductory conversation. But my being alive is not conditional on a place. In French they have *vivre* and *habiter*; in German *leben* and *wohnen*. In English, an immensely rich language, we have suppressed the distinction between being alive on the one hand and dwelling/abiding/residing on the other. Current usage has only the verb *to live*, as if being alive depended on being contained within four walls. Only in Scotland where they use the word "to stay", does a distinction remain.

But this merging of meaning has more than a linguistic significance. Increasingly, an address is used to define identity. Access to credit, a bank account, and to any number of public services, such as public libraries and bus passes, depend on it. Think how many times you have been asked for your address, indeed all the addresses of the past three years. Why is it anybody's business? Why has it become a marker of worth?

And what does it say about those who cannot provide one? "No fixed abode" has become a phrase of opprobrium. In newspaper reports of court cases, "NFA" immediately casts a suspicious light on the defendant, as if the lack of a fixed address equals fecklessness, if not an automatic admission of guilt.

I have an address, therefore I am? All the more so if we actually own our residence. Then, we are credit-worthy; we have an asset and can provide collateral. Increasingly, in the West, houses are about money. For those that own them, houses, rather than work, have become our money-makers; over the past fifteen years or so they have accrued monetary value at a rate that is hard to believe. Monopoly money, usually meaningless since, if we sold the house, we would only have to pay a similar amount for another. But, even when the housing market is buoyant, a home is not a milch-cow. When times are hard, perhaps we catch a glimpse of the truth that lies behind all the consumer-babble, the truth that home is actually something completely different.

So, apart from shelter, what makes a home in material terms?

Furnishing a first home or a son's or daughter's student flat gives one a pretty good idea of the basics needed to live our daily lives. A bed to sleep on, a cooker to cook on, table and chairs to sit at, a coffee table to put things on, a wardrobe and chest of drawers to put our clothes in, a TV to entertain us. Plus crockery, cutlery, pots and pans. And the furnishings – paint or wallpaper, carpet, curtains or blinds. Basic necessities. Except that, seeing how other people live, one can see that many of these are not necessities at all. We can live well with a mat on the floor, cushions not chairs, a rail instead of a wardrobe. I well remember the bookshelves we had as students made out from bits of wood separated by bricks. And in Bangladesh I watched my middle-class hostess squatting on the floor, chopping herbs on a block. The result was a superb, subtle fragrant array of dishes – and not a garlic press or even a kitchen table in sight.

We forget how recent some seemingly essential constituents of modern living are. Computers, television, electricity. Even in the UK, as late as the 1980s, a woman in a Cornish village said, "I've waited all my life to have a flush toilet." And recently a man, now in his sixties, told me that in the farmer's cottage where he lived as a child, the only light for the first eleven years of his life was from a candle. When I stayed with a French family in the early 1960s, theirs was one of the few farms locally to have

7

electricity. In many countries, it is still usual to live without any of what we would consider the basic amenities. Four out of ten people in the world have no sanitation – not even a bucket.

Under the heading "A Gift to be Simple", the novelist Susan Hill invited readers of her blog to list the things without which they would not like to live – for well-being, not necessity. For necessity she assumes "a roof over my head, food and fresh running water, the means of keeping myself and my clothes and house clean, heating and lighting and appropriate medicines if I am ill". Among such items as "chocolate" and "spectacles", suggestions from one reader include "wind and water-tight living space" and from another "somewhere warm and dry and safe to sleep (a bivvi bag, a tarp and a sleeping bag in some woods away from prying eyes would do me); something to keep my stuff dry and secure". Most agree that they would happily do without most of what they own.

So, maybe it's more about conditions than objects. Warmth in a cold climate; security (a door that closes and ideally locks); places that are dry, light, comfortable and, for many of us, reasonably quiet – although there are others who are happy with noise.

But how much more we have! Our houses have become shrines to material prosperity; as we have become recently and uncomfortably aware, they are our biggest investment; we spend long hours of our lives and much of our income looking after them. Where the house is and how big it is are not only about the practicalities of getting to work, or the number of people we need to house, but about status. There is social pressure to progress to something bigger, better, and in a "more desirable" location. "Location, location, location", the estate agent's watchword. And about 300,000 English households now have a second home in England (not to mention overseas).

Why are the English so obsessed with their houses and gardens? Television schedules are crammed with programmes about finding the house of our dreams, doing up our houses, always with money centre-stage. The increase – or decrease – in the price of housing and the evils of estate agents are everyday topics of conversation. And on bank holidays the DIY super-stores are crammed with home improvers.

For our investment is not only in the house itself, but in the furnishings and in its contents, which may change according to fashion or as we become more affluent. Not only the condition but the appearance of the building we live in preoccupies a large part of our time. What colour shall we paint the bathroom, what kind of tiles on the floor? The barrage of advertising on bill-boards, newspapers, magazines, TV and radio seduces us into wanting or "needing" more and more. The number of objects that we "cannot do without" grows all the time. During power cuts a woman in the USA wrote about having to do without her clothes dryer. In desperation, she draped clothes over shrubs and bushes in her garden, and was astonished to find that "it worked".

And our obsession is both voyeuristic and competitive. "Keeping up with the Joneses" is an international pastime. We are fascinated by the houses of celebrities, or of people that we know. In the UK the film director, Michael Winner, talks compet-itively of the £5 million he has spent on his 46-bedroom and seven-bathroom house, a big place for someone who hates enter-taining. In California luxury doghouses, based on their owners' houses, complete with running water, art and furniture, are for sale at £25,000.

Some very large houses in the States often have several kitchens, because the main one is too far to walk to from some parts of the house. In South Africa, Peter visited his sister's house, so large that he felt his whole house in England would fit into their bedroom. Seeing some binoculars on the window sill, he said that he wished he had brought his with him for bird-watching.

"Oh, those aren't for birds; it's so Ralph can watch television." The fixed TV was on a wall so far away that her husband needed binoculars to watch it.

Security

"An Englishman's home is his castle," and increasingly, not only in England, it's a fortified one.

There are few countries in which there is not a large gap between rich and poor, and in many – particularly the USA and UK – the gap is widening. The more unequal the society, the greater the fear of crime. Even in San Jose, the capital of Costa Rica, simple little houses in the suburbs are separated from the street by barred cages. On a hot evening occupants sit in their forecourt inside them like animals in a zoo. In Antigua, Guatemala, my mother's cousin used to have an armed guard; in Johannesburg, South Africa, a friend checks with the guard before she drives home from work. Her previous car, driven by a friend, was taken away at gunpoint not so long ago, so the fear is not unfounded.

The more we have, the more fearful and vulnerable we feel ourselves to be, and the more we pay in protection and insurance. And the more we separate ourselves. Walls, locks, bars, alarms, gated residences, razor wire, guards, dogs: all are part of a multi-million business based on property and fear. Even going to the bathroom at night can be hazardous. Twenty years ago, I remember staying in my uncle's bungalow in Geneva. Rooms radiated off a central hallway and, at night, the hallway was taken up by two large Doberman dogs that growled at any approach. The twenty-first-century equivalent was related to me by Peter who recently stayed in a house where the lasers in the bedroom, hall and bathroom had to be turned off for his nocturnal visits to the loo. "But don't on any account", said his hostess, "go into the kitchen." Some security systems are so sophisticated that when a property is left vacant, photos of possible intruders are automatically sent electronically to absent owners. A phone call to the security firm will send an armed response team who will shoot to kill. In South Africa, Peter says, the profits made from the security business are beginning to outweigh the wish to combat crime.

In its most extreme form security, and separation, are exemplified by gated estates, with controlled check-point entrances for pedestrians and cars, and characterised by a closed perimeter of walls and fences. For larger estates, it may not be necessary for residents to leave the area for most day-to-day activities. Tony, on returning to his native South Africa, found to his dismay that the entire village he grew up in had been gated. Shops were on the outside but the population of over a thousand people, complete with school, cemetery and church were enclosed. Locked up.

In the USA, where 11% of all new housing developments even in the mid-90s fell into this category, such estates are often called gated "communities" but a residential development based on possessiveness and the view that the world is a dangerous place, and closed off from the neighbouring area, calls into question the meaning of the word "community". Sharing and hospitality imply an open door.

High levels of security in cities such as Johannesburg where violent crime is a daily reality may be realistic; in Britain, said Mike, it's ridiculous. Living in the small town of Marlow on Thames, he mentioned a park across the river that had been gated for its residents. There had been some attempt to gate the group of houses in which he lives, but residents resisted it. They have no wish to be separated from their neighbours, imprisoned in a gilded cage.

The search for a perfect home

Often, when travelling from one place to another, passing villages and towns on the way, I wonder what makes someone live in a particular house. With all the houses in the world, why that one? Why live in that particular place?

In fact, choices may not be so numerous. Considerations may have to include being near work, near the family, what's available, what's big or small enough, near shops, what one can afford. Compromises have to be made – a busy road, the wrong side of the village, a pokey kitchen. For those on the waiting list for a council flat, most will take what they can get.

House-hunting can be a stressful business. A friend who lost her house during a previous financial crisis remembers house-hunting for a small place that they could now afford. Three times a week she travelled around by bus, "seeing all those roofs, and thinking 'there must be something for us to live in'". Having lived in a fine big house, she realised that "something for us to live in" is what matters: a shelter, a place of safety with our families.

House ownership

For many years house ownership in the West has been the most stable source of financial security. Except at times of financial crisis, houses have steadily been gaining in value, and governments have pressed for ever-increasing house ownership. To obtain a foot on the property ladder, people, couples, families invest their savings and often mortgage themselves to the hilt.

This is an interesting time to be writing about houses. The ramifications of the credit crunch have undermined our sense of financial security. We do not know if our pensions, our jobs, our houses, will be safe. But house ownership has never guaranteed wealth or financial security. Even before the current crisis, the Joseph Rowntree Foundation found that "half of all people living in poverty in Britain today are home-owners". In the UK and the US, companies have vied to lend often unrepayable amounts, with, as we know, catastrophic results. In the 1990s and the early years of this century, mortgage companies in the UK were offering to lend four or five times the buyers' joint incomes, sometimes up to 125% of the price of the property. When house prices fell, as in the early 1990s and in 2008, the availability of mortgages shrank so that even first-time buyers could not benefit from the lower prices. Existing owners are threatened by negative equity and, as interest rates and other housing costs rise, are increasingly unable to repay their loans. For those on the edge, even small increases threaten their ability to pay their bills. Unemployment goes up; the possibility of homelessness looms. In the UK repossessions in 2009 are expected to rise to 75,000; in the USA, the number of repossessions have doubled in a year. More than a million Americans have lost their houses in what has been called the worst housing crisis since the Great Depression.

As Mark Steel writes in the *Independent*:

Somehow this massive investment which for most people is not their shelter, but represents their life savings, security and everything, revolved around a huge gamble.

Henry Thoreau wrote along the same lines 150 years earlier:

When the farmer has got his house, he may not be the richer but the poorer for it, and it be the house that has got him (21).

In the UK advertisements for mortgages now carry with them a health warning, like that on cigarettes: "Your home may be repossessed if you fail to keep up payments on your mortgage."

Ownership can give security, both financially and emotionally. It can also be a millstone, and not just in material terms. One of the men I interviewed talked of a different dimension: "It's a trap to be wary of, the aspect of ownership. The spirit in which you live will be affected by your home. You can be trapped or enabled." One woman told me: "I had huge moral dilemmas about buying my first house when I divorced – 'property is theft', and all that. But I had to provide the kids with a home."

I spoke to two young men buying their first places to live. Olly rented for a while – it was an experimental, exploratory time, he says – but he has now bought his first flat. He felt it was time; it was a mark of being "grown up". Yes, he says, there is freedom in not owning somewhere, and he realises that he is lessening his own autonomy, but there is a different kind of freedom in having a say in your own life. He was bored with being dependent on others' good will.

Guy, in his thirties, moved out to the South of France about four years ago. Tired of being poor in London, he took the opportunity of an opening in his company to work in Nice. In so doing, he saved about £500 per month in fares and rent. He is now buying his first flat – something he could not afford to do in London. And, increasingly young people are moving out of London, or the UK, because they cannot afford to make homes for themselves here. Even in rural surroundings, the new generation increasingly cannot afford housing, and are leaving. The Joseph Rowntree Charitable Trust reported in 2008 that so few could afford housing that in some areas there was a danger that a whole generation would be lost. The report of the analysts, Hometrack, says that 28% of young people in work in the UK are unable to buy even their cheapest local properties.

It is no better in the States. According to Harvard's state of the nation's housing report, 2008,

Nowhere in America does a full-time minimum-wage job cover the cost of a modest two-bedroom rental at 30 percent of income. In the least affordable areas of the country, the income necessary to afford the fair market rent on a modest apartment, working 40 hours a week for 50 weeks a year – is now five times the current federal minimum wage.

A glimmer of hope appeared in the UK with the introduction of part-ownership which allows people to buy part of a house with the government or local council owning the rest. If they become wealthier, they can buy more of the property until they buy it all. It allows people who could not afford a full mortgage to get on the property ladder. But, inevitably, restrictions about income form gaps into which many families fall.

Renting

But does a home imply ownership? Not all countries see it as a priority. The number of people owning their houses in Australia is almost twice that of Switzerland, which like other rich nations in Western Europe has a low or moderate rate of owner-occupation. Some of the poorest, such as Greece and Portugal, have the highest. In Sweden, Ulla is only now, in her sixties, buying the flat in which she lives. She has delayed not because of poverty, but because renting gave her increased flexibility. And where she lives renting is much more the norm.

It used to be the norm in the UK too: in 1908 90% of the population rented their homes. A hundred years later, when renting in the UK and US accounts for less than a third of households, some wish it still was. Tim, who works in the charitable sector, feels it would be a perfect scenario if everyone rented. He would be happy in his renting if there was a tenancy that could not be so easily dissolved. If there was some security. Now in his thirties, he has been renting in London for about ten years, and has moved eight times. Now, his landlord wants to sell up and he and his wife will have to move again. His flat is rented through an agent who seems to forget that Tim and his wife are legal tenants and have rights. Tim says he cannot afford to buy. All the money goes on rent; it is impossible to save for a deposit. Even with two incomes they are not rich enough to afford to buy a flat – and not poor enough for social assistance.

The problem with renting, he says, is that "you can't influence the home you've got. You're just there, just existing. It's fine for a few years, but I don't ever anticipate having a home the way my mother does. A house with three bedrooms and a garden. I can't imagine where that would come from." It breeds, he says "a sense of apathy". His mother lives in a council house and has the right to live in it until she dies, and pass it on to a member of the family. That parental home feels like home – it's fixed; still there after thirty years.

And, he says, renting "has an impact on families". He and his wife have put off having a family because they can't afford the rent of a larger place. The only hope is to move out of London.

Trish rented with her family for many years in Canada before coming back to the UK and buying a house. She remembers that her husband would have been quite happy to continue renting. It didn't seem to bother him but, she said, "I felt very odd without my own home." Jo, in London, wonders whether she would feel the same about her flat if she didn't own it. As it is, she can alter anything she wants, do anything she wants with it.

Recently I spent about eighteen months renting in various places. I found myself quite content in a house that belonged to someone else, with someone else's furniture – it was not my responsibility. The freedom was much more important to me than attachment. Shedding responsibility was like breathing to the depths of my being.

But many living in privately rented accommodation do not have the same choices. In the 1970s the growth of council housing in the UK meant that many people on low incomes could find housing. Ten years later the "right to buy" council housing depleted the stock and meant a surge of those on low incomes who could not find anywhere to live, and of private landlords, buying to fill that need. They are in many cases absentee landlords, some of whom do not maintain their properties. In 2008 it was estimated that one million households in the UK live in properties below what local government define as "decent";

most privately rented accommodation is in deprived areas; and a high proportion of tenants are from vulnerable groups, such as elderly or disabled people. Many put up with substandard accommodation through fear of being evicted. Under the 1988 Housing Act fast track procedure, only two months' notice, and no explanation, are required. And, even apart from such "legal" possibilities, illegal repossession is frequent. With no notice given, a tenant is locked out and their possessions are left either inside the flat or on the pavement.

Houses of multiple occupation (HMOs), with increasing numbers of tenants crammed in, are a particular source of anxiety, especially to fire services who have expressed their concern about "potential death traps". There has been a rise in HMOs due to migration from Eastern Europe. Many of the residents do not know their rights, or are frightened to make a complaint.

Tenancy support officers manage to prevent some evictions, working with landlords and tenants to try to find a way forward; their aim "to make people feel safer in their own homes". Only 71 out of an estimated two million private landlords have joined the voluntary ombudsman scheme.

A BBC Radio 4 programme, *Policing the Landlords*, interviewed a number of tenants of private landlords. A woman with five children who had just lost her job, and whose benefits had not yet come through, had been threatened with having the door broken down if she didn't pay up by 3 pm that afternoon. A man with learning difficulties, we heard, has lived for two years with no hot water or heating. The meters have been torn out. He has been taken into hospital twice in the last month, and slept in his father's car. He is waiting for the court system to take action. Another whose ceiling has fallen in does not dare to complain for fear of being given notice. We also heard from a particular landlord who referred to his tenants as "vermin", saying "I deal with the scumbag element".

Social housing

Unlike the US, where its share is 2% and shrinking, social housing is an important part of the UK housing market. In 2006, council housing and housing associations represented over 18% of UK households, with four million people on the waiting list. The right to buy council houses, plus a much reduced building programme – in 2003 only half the number of social houses were built compared with 1995 – has meant an acute shortage, forcing many people into the vagaries of the privately rented sector, or into homelessness. The reliance on a points system ensures that only those with sufficient "deprivation" indicators are housed: not a good recipe for a healthy social mix.

However, the government has recently announced an intention to increase the number of social houses built per year, and, according to Rowntree, the quality of social housing is improving. Although some households live in poor conditions, the proportion of council homes which fail to meet the decent homes standard fell by a third between 1996 and 2004. And many local authorities are moving from giving prospective tenants just one choice of accommodation to a choice-based lettings system, based on a fortnightly leaflet offering available properties to people who can then "bid" with their points for properties that interest them.

Former England footballer Cyrille Regis was in council housing from the age of 5 until he was 21. To begin with, he said, they stayed in

> an old two-up, two-down property with an outside toilet and no bathroom. It had derelict houses on either side, but it was great for all the kids because we had access to gardens and more free space than we knew what to do with. Facilities were basic, and my mum and dad used to take us to the communal buildings in Paddington for our weekly bath, otherwise it was a case of washing and getting clean in the kitchen.

A few years later the council knocked down the whole road and gave us a flat [with]... four bedrooms and an inside toilet and bathroom – it was brand new and it seemed like heaven. This typifies one of the great things about social housing: the constant regeneration, and even these fantastically modern interlinking flats built only in the 70's have now been demolished and replaced by new developments (www.24dash.com/news/ Housing).

Estates acquire reputations, often based on the behaviour of a small minority of residents, and the reputation can be self-perpetuating. The propinquity of such estates might even lower the prices of private property in the area. One resident in 2004 talked of her estate as "a dump and that's being polite...you're ashamed of telling people where you live. You're on the bus and you want to stay on and go straight through" (Tunstall, 24).

Others made happy homes even on the same estates. According to Rebecca Tunstall, lecturer in housing at the London School of Economics, who has made a study of twenty estates in Britain over several generations,

Most estates did not show a clear trend of declining overall resident experience over estate lifetimes, but rather a complex series of ups and downs for residents as individuals and collectively (*ibid.*).

Measurement of housing satisfaction is necessarily narrow and cannot take into account the subtle diversities of need and expectation.

Ideal home
Good architecture is what makes us thrive, not survive.
Alain de Botton

A few years ago my partner and I spent several nights alone in the Western Desert in Egypt. A Land Rover dropped us off with water supplies, food and blankets, and as it receded into the distance, we surveyed the vast expanse of sand and rock around us. "Right," we said, pointing in various directions, "we'll sleep here; we'll eat there, and we'll go up the hill for the loo." Such simple needs; absolute choice in the placing of our "home" for the duration. Generally speaking, of course, we don't have such choices.

So, what kind of housing will make us thrive?

The orientation of houses is seen in many cultures to be key to the happiness of its inhabitants. It has recently been discovered that each ancient Amazonian community had an identical road, pointing north-east to south-west, which was connected to a central plaza. The roads were always oriented this way in keeping with the mid-year summer solstice. In the practice of Feng Shui ("wind and water"), practitioners use a special compass to locate houses and tombs where the energies are in harmonious balance. In this practice, the placing and orientation of houses and the objects within them are key in the promotion of positive energies and the creation of a beautifully balanced environment.

The use of local building materials is natural and appropriate in many contexts. The rich potential of this approach has been described by the architect, Laurie Baker, who lived and worked for many years in rural India.

I suppose it took many years before I really understood and wholeheartedly believed that wherever I went I saw, in the local indigenous style of architecture, the results of thousands of years of research on how to use only immediately-available, local materials to make structurally stable buildings that could cope with the local climatic conditions, with the local geography and topography, with all the hazards of nature (whether mineral, vegetable, insect, bird or animal), with the possible hostility of neighbours, and that could accommodate all the requirements of local religious, social and cultural patterns of living. This was an astounding, wonderful and incredible achievement which no modern, twentieth century architect, or people I know of, has ever made.

I learnt more about the more acceptable local materials, with new (to me) ways of using burnt brick, stone, tiles and timber. I also used new kinds of mortar and plaster and, as much as possible, tried to design my buildings in such a way that they would not be offensive or unacceptable to my real clients, the users of the buildings, and so that they would fit in with the local styles and not be an offence to the eyes of the people with whom I had chosen to live (http://lauriebaker.net/work).

Sadly, though, architect-designed buildings are rarely available to the poor. For the majority in rural India and other developing areas, houses made from local materials do not necessarily stand up well to local weather conditions. Rattan houses in Madagascar leak; mud houses in South Africa are subject to disintegration in the rain. Corrugated iron roofs are a luxury but, even weighted down by stones, often blow off in a storm.

Christopher Alexander's view of the architect's role reaches far beyond bricks and mortar. "It is the architect's task to render vivid to us who we might ideally be." It is about "the question of the values we want to live by – rather than merely of how we want things to look... We depend on our surroundings obliquely to embody the moods and ideas we respect, and then to remind us of them... What we seek, at the deepest level, is inwardly to resemble, rather than physically to possess, the objects and places that touch us through their beauty" (1977: 13, 73, 107, 152).

How Alexander goes about these tasks is in a profound and innovative philosophy that has proved influential to a generation of architects. In his seminal works, *The Timeless Way of Building* and *A Pattern Language*, he sets out a philosophy that cannot easily be defined in words:

It is a process which brings order out of nothing but ourselves; it cannot be attained, but it will happen of its own accord, if we only let it...

It is a process through which the order of a building or a town grows out directly from the inner nature of the people, and the animals, and plants, and matter which are in it.

It is a process which allows the life inside a person, or a family, or a town, to flourish, openly, in freedom, so vividly that it gives birth, of its own accord, to the natural order which is needed to sustain this life...

This quality can only come to life in us when it exists within the world that we are part of. We can come alive only to the extent the buildings and towns we live in are alive. The quality without a name is circular: it exists in us, when it exists in our buildings; and it only exists in our buildings, when we have it in ourselves. To understand this clearly, we must first recognize that what a town or building is, is governed, above all, by what is happening there (1979: ix, 7, 62, original italics).

Alexander then gives examples of the kind of events, large and small, that fill the lives of people and places – hurricanes, the birth of a child, a friend dropping in, and so on.

If this approach sounds abstract, Alexander has expressed it in thousands of pages of the most tangible and precise detail, from the dimensions and placing of an alcove to the relationship of a house to its surroundings:

Connect the building to the earth around it by building a series of paths and terraces and steps around the edge. Place them deliberately to make the boundary ambiguous – so that

it is impossible to say exactly where the building stops and earth begins (1977: 787).

Not only does a harmonious building come from this nameless quality in ourselves, he says, but it also depends on *"certain patterns of relationships among the elements"* of the building that define it.

Even an empty building is more than its structure. Different buildings feel different, and that is particularly true of buildings designed for people to live in. These feelings are personal, of course, and what repels one might attract another. But there are some dwelling places that are welcoming, peaceful. It's often to do with the people who live there, who have made of it a home, somewhere hospitable, an extension of their own serenity. But it's also true of empty buildings: some have a better atmosphere than others. There is a feel beyond what it looks like and who lives there. When house-hunting, people will usually be drawn to particular buildings for indefinable reasons. They talk of "vibrations". I used to live in a very attractive three-bedroom maisonette, with French windows opening out on to a pretty enclosed garden; it was in a convenient and friendly area – theoretically ideal. But, strangely, the office that I bought at the same time, and in which I now dwell, felt more attractive from the beginning; I felt more "at home" in it. When my brother came here for the first time, I was expecting criticism of its small size, its emptiness. But he said that it had a good feel, indeed a better one than my previous flat. So it was not just me that felt it.

The same is true in reverse: there are places that have an uncomfortable, even an "evil" feel. House hunters will be repelled, for no reason that they can understand. Often it will turn out that the house has been witness to scenes of violence, abuse, pain or sorrow. An architect told me of a house where hard-headed builders and plumbers refused to go down to the two lower floors: they felt they were haunted. On her first visit she too felt something in the dark, old house – an unloved feeling – but the Chinese owners dismissed the feelings until they came to live there, when they too were loath to descend to the basement. Apparently, the house next door had brought in an exorcist to deal with a "presence" in their basement; maybe, as the architect said, the ghost had moved next door! Later she discovered that a murder had taken place a couple of doors away and that prostitution had been rife in the area. In the same way that many feel that places of worship used over centuries have a sense of holiness, so ugliness and suffering can make their mark. Bricks, perhaps, have memory.

Peopled, a house or flat will reflect the changing needs of its occupants. Consider "the spare room", if there is one: a bedroom used, perhaps, for occasional guests. It might double up as the venue for hobbies and activities such as dressmaking or painting; it might house the computer, a drum kit or the household junk. When a baby is expected, it may be decorated in soft colours as a nursery; when one of the household starts working more often from home, it will be turned into an office. The more flexible the space, the more it allows for continuing occupancy during the changing times of family life.

Home increasingly is also a workplace. With technological advances, more and more people are enabled to work from the place where they also dwell – it can be cheaper for the employer, and more convenient for the person concerned. There are dangers of isolation, but at least some work hours spent in an environment of one's choosing can be a boon, especially if it enables parents to spend more time with small children. As someone who ran a business from home for ten years, I know how important it is to keep the "work" space separate, and to maintain boundaries about the time spent working: not to open the work mail at weekends, to have a separate phone line and email address. When colleagues or work visitors enter the "home" space, it can impinge adversely on other members of the family.

Sometimes there is no choice about working at home. Self-employed people may not have the resources to pay for the overheads of a separate working space. The women starting businesses with whom I worked in the East End of London found it hard to have time and space for their work amidst the demands of family and often in confined spaces.

In early 2008, the BBC broadcast a series on "the history of the home", a series about changing taste. It coincided with the centenary of the Ideal Home Show, the largest "home" show in the world, that throughout the 20th century and into this one has documented the love affair between the British public and their houses: a history set against a background of social change and technological advance.

Much has changed in those hundred years, but "in 1908 as now," the catalogue told us,

visitors queued patiently to view the exquisitely furnished houses and to tour a unique landscaped garden. Stands became rooms with all the merchandise available for sale – offering the opportunity for people to see the latest designs for luxury living…

Technological developments gathered pace throughout the 1920s and 1930s and …the event became a focal point for the housewife to view the latest in household technology. Throughout the 1930s building was Britain's chief industry, and the suburbs began to spread. Mortgages were becoming more accessible and more people than ever before bought their first home.

In 2008 I queued to see the "dream house and guest house": a show house, which was "to present an exceptional example of modern living for the twenty-first century for an affluent family". The house was meant to represent "simple comfortable living. Space is the key word; an inspirational interior that flows with ease from room to room." I found the house certainly for the affluent but far from simple. It was hard-edged and cold, lacking spirit. Despite allowing space for a guest wing, the warmth of hospitality was entirely lacking in the white laminate shelving, the clean hard lines. I was reminded of a television programme from many years before that profiled individuals and their houses. The episode that came to mind was one that showed the house of an architect who would not allow his wife to have curtains in their house. It would spoil the style, the overall look, his vision for the house. Nothing to do with relationship and understanding or providing a loving home for all who lived in it. Like the show house, it was sterile and unforgiving.

Unlike the show house, however, were the endearingly old-fashioned salesmen at the fair with microphones lauding the attractions of the magic mop or kitchen equipment. Elsewhere, a salesman sprawled gloomily on one of his products, a beanbag, awaiting customers at his stall. Videos, hi-tech, yes, but nothing to beat the sales patter of a real person. And a lot of opportunities for people to ask questions, "consult the expert", have a cup of tea. Socially, technologically, financially, much has changed, but some things stay humanly the same.

And it was on this human level, I saw, that the show appealed. For among the visitors there was a family atmosphere: young couples furnishing their first house, perhaps; older couples with children – a day out with laughter, cooing at babies, and negotiating choices. Because, whatever the changing styles before them, and the promotion of what is in fashion, however insecure people are about their own taste, they will in the end express themselves in the context of their financial resources and the space available to them. One man I spoke to said he was not artistic: his house was the only place in which he could create beauty.

From cave art on, human beings have personalised the spaces in which they live. Even in temporary surroundings there is an urge to impose a pattern, a place to hang a coat, a towel, and a shelf for the clock or the toiletries. The need for familiarity, knowing where things are, goes deep in the human psyche. How much more so, then, in a place that is lived in, where its objects as well as its inhabitants have made their mark. Even in a row of characterless box-houses, or a block of identical flats, inhabitants will make them their own: curtains or blinds at the window; a window box or hanging basket; the colour of the front door. And inside, each house will be quite different. We all like to "read" the space with which someone surrounds themself. The books, the choice of music, the pieces of furniture and how they are placed in the room, and the choices of colour and lighting. This is where the consumer culture can lure our insecure selves into an endless search, an obsessive pursuit, of what we hope will impress. But for friends or visitors to the house, the ultimate in high design is less interesting than a quirky jug, Granny's somewhat tatty armchair or a child's shoe discarded on the stairs. We are drawn by things that express the individual self, the inner life. Pictures or ornaments that speak of other times or other places. Family history made manifest.

The architecture or placing of a house may well influence what happens in it, but it is what goes on within the walls that makes the difference – prayer, relationship, love or hatred – not the bricks and mortar themselves. When Karl's marriage broke up, he left home. He travelled round the country, visiting places in which he and his wife had been happy – often many years before – and rang her from each spot, trying to bring back what they had had in that place. But the relationship did not lie in the place, which had merely been a witness. And a relationship is fluid, not stuck in time and place.

Will Self refers to the complex relationship between buildings and our feelings in and about them. He writes of "that most strange of things: the gradual accretion of memories, and sensations, and memories of those sensations, that perfuse mere bricks and mortar and possessions, to end up, quite inevitably, creating a genuine sense of home" (Smolan and Erwitt in the *Independent*, 7 June 2008).

A physical home is a context for living and exploration: a place to feel safe in and step out from in confidence, energy and love.

3

Broken circles

Homeless

Annual Commemoration Service
for those who died homeless (in London) during the year

St Martin-in-the-Fields
8th November, 2007

A full church. Professionals working with homeless people and homeless people themselves, mourning their friends, part of their community.

One by one, the reading of 105 names. A few women, a sprinkling of foreign names. Some life stories.

A Canadian who came to this country to start a new life. He was a trained chef and got a good job. When he developed muscular dystrophy he lost his job and became homeless.

A man who had been in the army for many years and ran his life – and helped to run St Martin's soup kitchen – with military precision. I remembered meeting him when he lived under Waterloo Bridge, and took us on a conducted tour of Cardboard City. He was 79 when he died, and had been homeless for over twenty years.

A Polish man, highly educated, who came here for a new life after his divorce. Alcohol took over. He was badly beaten up not long before he died, brain damaged, and never really recovered.

"Come to him, to that living stone, rejected by men but in God's sight chosen and precious: like living stones be yourselves built into a spiritual house" (1 Peter 2. 4-6, 9-10).

We each held a stone. Most had a name on; some did not, to represent those who died, like the unknown soldier, without being recorded. And, thinking of Remembrance Day which fell a few days later, one man expressed the wish that we could have a national service for those who had died homeless. At the end of the service we placed our stones in a spiral in front of the altar.

Prayers. Homeless people trained by professional opera singers singing Carmen's flower song, with red roses, and

There's a place for us
Somewhere a place for us...

"Everyone has the right to a standard of living adequate for the health and well-being of himself and of his family, including food, clothing, housing" (Universal Declaration of Human Rights, Article 25, December 10, 1948).

In 1999 I went to Bangladesh. Before I went, people warned me of what to expect – Bangladesh is one of the poorest countries in the world. On arrival I told my host that "I did not know what poverty was till I came here".

The response was sharp: "It is harder to be homeless in a cold country than a hot one."

And hard it is. Imagine spending just one night on the streets. Am I allowed to be here? Will I be arrested? How to keep warm? How to keep safe, away from prying eyes? And my belongings, where can I put them? Cardboard to add warmth and pad the hardness of the pavement? Where can I pee? Do my teeth? Get a drink of water? Wash? And change/wash clothes? It is astonishing how many street homeless people cope, how clean they are. Yes, there are day centres which provide showers. But you need to know where they are and when they are open, how to find them when perhaps you don't know the city, and have no money for travel. And maybe there's a language problem. Not to mention mental health issues or drug or drink dependencies which can be caused by the stress of being homeless if they weren't there before.

Why do people become homeless in rich countries – in Europe, in the US, in Australia? According to Harvard's state of the nation's housing report in 2008, there are between 2.3 and 3.5 million homeless people each year in the States, including 600,000 families. Any of us could become homeless, but UK government and NGO statistics show that people are more likely to become so if they were in care as a child, have a mental illness or addiction, have been in the armed forces, have spent time in prison, are black or from another minority ethnic community, have migrated to this country from eastern or central Europe or arrived as an asylum-seeker.

In 2003 the Prison Reform Trust, the Big Issue and NACRO (National Association for the Care and Resettlement of Offenders) ran a campaign for prevention of homelessness for prisoners on release. In writing the scoping study for the campaign, I interviewed prisoners, prison staff and members of NGOs working in prisons, and found how little work was being done to prevent homelessness on release. Efforts have been made since then, and some progress made but, even so, the number of prisoners helped in any given area is small, and still almost a third are released with no fixed abode. Around 20% of women and 14% of men have been homeless before they go into prison – and nothing has changed for the better when they go out. How is a life to be transformed with no shelter, no security, and with family relationships scarred and often dislocated by imprisonment?

But homelessness is not confined to specific groups of "other" people. In 2008, the housing charity, Crisis, said that a quarter of the people using their services had had a stable home and work life before becoming homeless. One in five people in the UK described their housing situation as "unpredictable" – and that was before the credit crunch. Given the high levels of debt – the UK is one of the most indebted of nations – it is perhaps not surprising. Twelve thousand people were expected to declare themselves insolvent in 2008. An inner city priest said that we are all "just two pay cheques and a broken marriage away from homelessness". There is a rise in "white collar tramps". Homeless people are not "other". They are us.

It is important to remember that in recent times the sight of beggars on the streets of London is new. Poverty has always been with us, but street homelessness on the scale it is today jumped into being in the 1970s. When I was growing up in London, there were a few "tramps", usually middle-aged or elderly, "gentlemen of the road". It was only when benefits were taken away from the 16 to18 year olds that suddenly people were begging on the streets. It was – and is – deeply shocking that in one of the wealthiest countries in the world, a sight reminiscent of the poorest countries, or of Victorian times in our own country, should become so commonplace on our city streets.

How is it that we have to come to accept such destitution, such inequity? Not only to accept it, but treat those who suffer with such lack of compassion? Maybe it is because of our own fear. Our own need for safety and security is such that we wish to push away from ourselves as far as possible such a predicament and those that embody it. The slippery road is all too visible.

I think most passers-by either take the sight of homeless people so much for granted that they genuinely don't notice, or are so embarrassed and guilty that they don't know what to do. We all cope as best we can with the sense of inequality, guilt, embarrassment, uncertainty and suspicion that besets us at the sight of a beggar. What should I do? What good will a bit of money make – and how much is enough? What will he spend it on? How do I know he is genuine? Is it worse to risk being conned or to risk not helping someone in a desperate plight – for whatever reason? I once gave quite a lot of money to someone for a train fare, and learnt later that I had been cheated. I was initially cross, but had known I was taking a risk, and in the long run it didn't matter. He almost certainly needed it more than I did. Professionals working with homeless people here and in, for instance, India, advise us not to give to individuals, but to charities who help them, and in general I do not give money – partly, I suspect, from an innate meanness. In general I offer to buy a drink or something to eat. And always engage, meet people's eyes, ask how they are doing, have a communication with another human being.

I have only learnt to do this late in life, my understanding transformed by taking part in tea-runs for homeless people. Beforehand, I was full of nervous preconceptions about what I would find. Instead of being sneered at as a middle-class busybody, or threatened by a druggie, I found myself forming relationships with other human beings. Offering a young man a cup of tea instead of stepping over a bundle in a doorway transformed my understanding and dashed my preconceptions.

Strangely, "shelter" does not appear in all versions of Maslow's hierarchy of needs but, even at the physiological level, there are few needs that are not endangered by the lack of a home. Given the number of people who die on the streets, even breathing is under threat.

In Moscow, hundreds freeze to death each year. Just before Christmas 2007, the neglect of homeless people in Paris, with men freezing to death on the streets, made headlines and raised a political storm. In London, with the honourable exception of the those volunteering for church and charity shelters, the plight of those living on the streets in freezing weather meets with, it seems, sublime indifference. I live in central London and witness tides of shoppers sweeping past street homeless people in their quest for more and more acquisitions. At Christmas, in particular, I found the comparison intolerable. On one occasion I saw a group of about ten men converge on the rubbish sacks outside a sandwich shop in Regent Street: foraging, scavenging. What have we come to? One of the men I talked to said it was

33

freefalling. You hit the streets. It's miserably cold and depressing, it's lonely, it's scary – bloody scary on the streets, it really is. Everything is taken away from you. You haven't got no rights any more. Your life is worth nothing. Within a week you're a complete mess. You lose your dignity, your pride.

I talk daily to men and women sleeping rough. Those whose stories I hear are often new on the streets, isolated, with no idea of shelters or hand-outs – far from the popular image of the grasping beggar or dependency culture. One dark night, in heavy rain, I came across a homeless man sitting on Westminster Bridge. I commiserated with him about the weather.

He said: "Believe it or not, I'm a nurse."

"What on earth are you doing here?"

"I was on night duty one night, and they brought my mother in DOA [dead on arrival]. I cracked up, broke down, lost everything."

It could indeed be any of us. Most of the stories of particularly middle-aged men are of a marriage break-up. A man who leaves the house to the wife and kids, sure that he'd be fine, find somewhere else. Then depression set in, maybe drink took over, he lost his job, and ended up on the streets. It doesn't take much.

Some surmount their predicament with extraordinary cheerfulness. A *Big Issue* seller I spoke to the other day in the heart of London's theatreland told me that he dog-sits for one of his regular customers; living in a hostel the rest of the time. "I can't have a pet, so I have a part-time one."

I expressed pleasure that he was no longer on the streets: "Anything is better than that."

"Well," he said, "I met some great people. Everyone: the street sweepers, the police, the doorkeepers – I got given tickets for the theatre a couple of times." His attitude – "I'm either mad or a great optimist" – attracted a positive response from all he met.

It is a rare experience. One man I talked to said: "The worst thing about being homeless is how passers-by treat you." Abuse, spitting, kicking, being beaten up. Government strictures and the tabloid press have persuaded the public that those without homes deserve not compassion but contempt. Sally, outside All Soul's church in central London said: "It's awful, people keep coming and urinating at night – and they're not even homeless." Graham Walker wrote in the homeless magazine, the *Big Issue*, that abuse

> nails their fate to the streets. It affirms what you are already thinking about yourself. Trying to stand proud in the street is a huge ask for a homeless person and I've seen people take time out of their little world to go and abuse a homeless person and I'm convinced that abuse just keeps them there longer.

And the UK government believes in a firm hand. Although much of the Vagrancy Act 1824 has been repealed, it is still an offence to beg in any public place; also, for a person so convicted, to sleep in certain unoccupied premises or in the open air without giving a valid reason. Local authorities have a duty to house only according to certain limited criteria. Charities are increasingly constrained, especially if their main funding comes from government. Homeless people have to fit tick-boxes – not least of which is having to prove a local connection. It was only after protest from community organisations last year that Westminster Council withdrew plans to ban giving food out to people on the streets. Operation Poncho, a punitive initiative to reduce "vagrancy", was introduced in 2007 in the City of London. People are woken early each morning and told to move their belongings so that their sleeping place can be washed down. Apparently all the doorways targeted have been washed already, late the previous evening. Disrupting people's sleep, moving them on in the middle of the night, only serves to increase their fear and lack of self-confidence; it does nothing to help house them.

For homeless people on the streets of London, fear and security are about physical safety. Sleeping in groups is recommended by housing charities as a safer option, but many want to be on their own, often hiding away. In a rich country, it is shameful to be poor. In India, where there is extreme poverty and a great deal of street homelessness, people living on the street are rarely isolated. Even on the streets, most live in family groups; most have a sense of a village elsewhere that is "home".

Writing in the 1860s, Henry Mayhew said,

The first instinct of the well-to-do visitor is to breathe a thanksgiving (like the Pharisee in the parable) that "he is not as one of these".

But the vain conceit has scarcely risen to the tongue before the better nature whispers in the mind's ear, "By what special virtue of your own are you different from them? How comes it that you are well clothed and well fed, whilst so many go naked and hungry?" And if you in your arrogance, ignoring all the accidents that have helped to build up your worldly prosperity, assert that you have been the "architect of your own fortune", who, let us ask, gave you the genius or energy for the work?

Then get down from your moral stilts, and confess it honestly to yourself that you are what you are by that inscrutable grace which decreed your birthplace to be a mansion or a cottage rather than a "padding-ken", or which granted you brains and strength...

It is hard for smug-faced respectability to acknowledge these dirt-caked, erring wretches as brothers, and yet, if from those to whom little is given little is expected, surely, after the atonement of their long suffering, they will make as good angels as the best of us (443).

Ken is a young American, very tall, slim and good looking, with long fair hair, which he flicks back with a toss of his head. Laid back, laconic. He is also a recovering alcoholic who was formerly homeless.

"Home? It's always been tricky for me." When Ken was young the family moved around the USA a good deal. "When I moved out at 18, my mum rented out my room." He didn't have a secure feeling of home, or place – or indeed, in a bigger sense, of personal identity. "Even now, when people ask, 'Where are you from?' I think, 'Yes, where?'" He says he has always had a "lack of home identity", and tries to create it from time to time.

Ken had dreams of being a world traveller. He was "looking for something". He came to the UK in 1991, worked in his aunt's restaurant in Devon, went back and forth to France, hitchhiking, for three years. Devon is the place he has lived for the longest – on and off for twelve years – and is "the place I go back to, have family, my important junk, somewhere always there for me".

From the time he came to the UK, he was drinking a lot. It made interacting with people easier. "I had a general feeling of being awkward in my skin. It wouldn't have mattered where I lived. It was me that was unsettled, ill at ease." In 1995 he went to Nottingham to study. It was his first attempt to settle down. "I felt I was under pressure from my family to 'get serious'." He took a job with a bank, hated it, and went back to Devon.

He returned briefly to New Mexico, because his grandmother was dying. "She was part of my American identity. With no father, my grandparents were an important part of my life." Then his aunt sold the restaurant. While he was away, all his stuff was moved to a cottage. Ken felt lost – the restaurant had been his focus – and he moved to London to live with a girl.

I hadn't given myself time to breathe; didn't know London. The drinking followed me to London – it became a problem very quickly. We split in 2003, and I became homeless. I thought it was depression, didn't realise it was the drink. I went back to Exeter for a year. Life took a dive. I'd been a functioning alcoholic so long, and now I couldn't work any more. I lived in supported private accommodation, sharing a house for those with low-level support needs. I didn't acknowledge that I was homeless. I considered "I was having a nervous breakdown". I couldn't afford to drink out, so I drank in with others. I got kicked out. Then I was dossing with a friend, a heroin addict. I didn't know how to sort myself. More and more squatting with heroin addicts – they steal all your stuff. We had a row; six heroin addicts ganged up on me, and I became a rough sleeper. I slept under a railway arch under a support like a fireplace. There was plenty of wood around and I made fires which warmed the bricks. I made a floor from cardboard. I was drinking cider.

I chose to be alone. I was isolated, quite scared, timid, felt ashamed. I finally realised I was homeless. Didn't tell my family, not even my aunt, twenty miles away. Pride. I was on the dole. I had never been before: we were a family who worked. I had a lot of support. I used to go to a drop-in centre, went to classes, used the computer.

In January 05 I came to London. I was "properly homeless", carrying bags, with dirty fingernails [he looks at his nails]. I accepted the situation. The street scene in Camden, nice people. Took me in very quickly. Sat with a fag and a bottle of cider. People kept coming up to me, talking to me, asking if I was all right. There was a sense of freedom. Used to worry about money. Now I couldn't do anything, so I didn't worry. Soup kitchens. American church. I was given a chicken leg and a loaf of bread by someone who used to be homeless. I signed on, got a doctor, got things sorted quite quickly. You used to have to have been six months in the place to use the night shelter. I was told to lie or people lied for me.

For a month I went from the night shelter to a day centre, to the canal, to the library. I washed in public toilets in the early morning. I had plans for a hostel, for a job.

He stayed ten months in one hostel. "Living with 160 crazy people; 100 on heroin". He almost left several times, but wanted to stay in the system. "It was a good facility with good staff, ratio 15:1, staffed 24 hours a day."

It took being completely homeless to realise that drink was a problem. Ken eventually went into rehab: and then to AA, which he still attends on a regular basis, and from there got a flat. "When I got the flat in November 06, it took a month to sink in. I'd been moving all the time: hostel, rehab. It was the first place of my own."

Ken is now doing a counselling course and volunteers at a Providence Row day centre, mentoring, befriending homeless people at the point at which they first access services.

I hated my life; something needed to happen. It was the experience I needed. I don't miss it but I look back on it as an experience. I was homeless, so I'll always be part of that. The idea of home is still something I'm sorting out for myself.

Mike, who has worked with homeless people for many years, feels that he has only met two men who didn't want a home. One of them was ex-army, who had worked up through the ranks to become a captain. His expertise was in undercover work, and he had got used to sleeping rough. He slept under Blackfriars Bridge in London, and commanded respect from the other street homeless people; he even had a bank account and took the occasional job. He had friends with whom he could stay occasionally: he had it all sorted. For four years he travelled, walking all over South America. A house would have been an impediment.

But he is an exception. The vast majority of people are homeless through circumstance and necessity. If someone says it's through choice, we need to look at what other choices – an abusive partner? – are on offer. The causes of homelessness are not purely material, and nor are the needs or solutions. Even if someone lacks the basics, that does not mean that the basics are all they need. There's a common preconception among the housed that those without houses should be grateful for anything: out-of-date sandwiches and scruffy second-hand clothes are frequent offerings. A friend in Canada was collecting clothes to give to poor families and had to throw away a lot of what she was donated. Unwashed, torn, good enough for "them", it would seem. Having lost so much, the right to choice in small matters is all the more important: white or brown bread, how much sugar in the tea. People may accept what is given from need, but giving choices bestows a little of the dignity so easily stripped by circumstance and the attitude of passers by. Self-esteem is one of the crucial building blocks of recovery.

Fi Tillman graphically evokes the pain of street homelessness and what led to it:

> Pavement is rock solid. Okay it's cold and rough, but it's reliable, it won't reject or abandon you, it doesn't...tell you that you're worthless, it doesn't leave you with tainted bruises, or acidic reminiscences. So here my roots can at last grow, filter through into the cracks and drop deep down into the subterranean, out of sight (Ephraums, 81).

Temporary housing

Of course a home is not just a roof, and the roofless are only the tip of a very large iceberg. An unknown number of people "sofa-surf" (living on friends' floors or spare rooms), indulge in "skippering", (breaking into empty houses without heating or electricity, pretending not to be there), or "squat" in empty properties in more "official" ways, sometimes with the council's blessing. I met one man who was skippering in a house with no windows – and when I asked, no heating. He's not on a waiting list, as he moves around a lot and "others with children need it more".

In England alone, the use of temporary rather than permanent housing for homeless people has more than doubled in the last decade and there are 79,500 households trapped in temporary accommodation, with families often living for years in overcrowded, damp and mice-infested rooms.

Antonina's story gives the flavour:

We went to Homeless Families in Manchester and we were all put in a bed and breakfast there for four, five weeks. They did find a room, but it was one room for all of us, seven of us. There were three lots of bunk beds and a broken pull-down bed. That's what it was. A shared kitchen, shared bathroom and toilets and everything and so it was a really, really, big shock.

David, because he'd just started high school, he had to get two buses at half past seven in the morning by himself. And then we had to get two buses a bit later on with Katie and Robert to take them to school.

. The children weren't allowed to play out, they had to be in their rooms for seven o'clock at night. There were no facilities for them to play. We used to take them out an awful lot, down to me mum's and I used to find, especially in the six weeks holiday that I went somewhere with them every day, so they weren't stuck in that room all the time.

Everybody was tarred with the same brush. In other words, they got this picture of what a homeless person is, and nobody can be outside the mould. We're one of the luckier ones, but there's going to be people out there now that are going into homeless families. We're on the tail end of it now, we are coming through and I think we are one of the luckier families because we've had a lot of support from my mum. I just think that people should be aware of all this. Because nobody has any idea, you don't know what it's going to be like, it's scary anyway. Because I've lost me home and I don't know what's going to happen next. You're nobody, you become nothing and nobody and that's how we felt (www.Shelter.org.uk)

Hostels

Founded in 1860 in the City of London, Providence Row is one of the UK's oldest charities for homeless people. From the very beginning it was open to everyone regardless of age, sex, nationality or creed: the first non-sectarian shelter for the poor in London. Their mission? To provide a place of refuge for anyone who is vulnerable or destitute so that they can transform their lives.

A few years ago Providence Row had a substantial refurbishment, with money raised partly by the charity and partly from government. Since one third of their income comes from government, they have to conform to certain criteria but, although they work closely with the local council, they still cater for homeless people from elsewhere. Placed as it is on the borders of the business centre of London and Tower Hamlets, one of the poorest areas in the country, it naturally attracts people from a wide area.

Providence Row runs a day centre that caters for about 120 men and women a day, providing food, clothing, showers, support and advocacy services, referring to housing, detox centres, and to other specialist agencies. The first hour of the day is dedicated to the needs of rough sleepers. In the afternoons they run classes for art, photography, literacy, and for over 50s. They have dedicated workers for people with mental health issues, drug and drink dependency, and for women. They also have a hostel on site with forty bedsits and eighteen self-contained flats.

Although the government has invested a good deal in the refurbishment of hostels over the past few years, their quality varies considerably. Some feel like correctional institutions, and many have an undercurrent of violence. Many street homeless people talk of their belongings being stolen, being beaten up because they don't take drugs: the security of a hostel user cannot be guaranteed. There are many mentally ill people in the hostel system. People often stay on the streets because they are frightened, cannot cope with their vulnerability in a hostel. They feel safer on the streets.

Andy has been on the streets for two and a half years. He is waiting for a hostel that will take him and his dog.

Mark is in a hostel. "It's not so bad," he says. They turn people out if they become violent, but if the temperature drops below -5°, they are allowed back in to sleep on the floor in the hallway.

Not only is there often no room in a hostel, but there is a shortage of move-on accommodation.

Mike, who had worked for years with street homeless people, became so angry at hearing that there was no move-on accommodation that he decided to do something about it. The formation of Homelink, one of the first rent guarantee schemes, was the result.

Mike describes "the most spectacular change" that he witnessed. They picked up a couple living in a room about 9 x 9, with a window high up on the wall in "a terrible hostel" near the City of London. The couple were in their twenties, troubled, poor and dishevelled. The woman had cancer; her partner wanted to do his best by her. The flat they were taken to was on a hill: a "decent flat"; done up with care: a nurturing space with attention to the little things. On the stairs, there were little colourful knick-knacks; at the top there was a glorious view over London from the back window. The couple had brought with them all their possessions, in one carrier bag.

Homelink currently operates, with its seven staff, from upstairs offices in a church in East London. Clients are referred from two London boroughs, and the team work with local landlords and estate agents to get people into privately rented accommodation. They then support their clients for the following six months, helping them with any problems they might have with the landlord, or on practical matters. Many formerly homeless people have little or no experience of managing their own place, and the support is very necessary. Many also have little understanding of their rights, which can be exploited by landlords or agents who themselves often have little idea of housing law.

As Natalie, the tenancy sustainment officer, herself with experience of homelessness, wrote,

> Much more than the practicalities, it is the mental strain insecurity places on an individual and the way this impacts negatively in so many areas of your life, that is the most damaging aspect of being homeless. Too often such individuals are left bewildered long after being housed.

Few are referred to Homelink straight from the streets; most are currently in hostels, as is Len, whom I met on the day he came to be registered.

Len is a recovering alcoholic, and lives in an abstinence hostel run by the Salvation Army. He has been there over two years, and finds it difficult. The uncertainty has been hard to handle: never knowing the next step. There were few allocations to council housing, and the Salvation Army wanted to send him out of London. He repeats his gratitude, and says "he wouldn't want to knock it" but the key workers, he says, are not trained to deal with recovery, and his daughter, aged twelve, is not allowed to visit. He had previously spent a few months in prison. "I could have avoided it, but felt it was somewhere I could go, hide away, give me time to think." When he was referred to the hostel under a new move-on scheme he didn't really know what he was getting into.

"Home?" he queried. "It's comfort, somewhere to live. Just living in it. I'd like to say security, but I don't know about that sometimes. Somewhere safe. A place I can be responsible. Everyone should have a home. It's everything, in't it, a home?"

The O of community

There are numerous initiatives to help and to support homeless people in Britain: day centres, hostels, specialist agencies to deal with addiction, training, employment possibilities, art classes, a mobile library, as well as housing. Sometimes an individual or a group of people will go beyond offering services: to involve themselves in the plight of others; to create a place of inclusion and equality.

For fifteen years Kath ran St Martin's hostel in south London. Although the eight-bedded hostel had no communal area, she tried to run it as a therapeutic community, tried to replicate family for those who had no experience of "normal" family life. The men came from fragmented homes, and had a multiplicity of problems from paedophilia to severe mental health issues and drink and drug problems; even one man with Huntingdon's chorea. Men were damaged, often bitter; rooms were trashed, police sometimes had to be called in. Kath lived in a flat on the premises, always on call. She tried to give the men some experience of doing things together: arranged outings, held a Christmas party to which she invited many who had left; gave some intimations of family life. All men were interviewed before they came; the hostel's book of policies included rules of confidentiality and a ban on violence. Some men stayed years, but most applied for resettlement after a while, and some did successfully settle in council flats, even old people's homes or other therapeutic communities. Sources of housing dried up as time went on and there were fewer council properties available. Some men couldn't cope with unsupported independent living, and ended up back on the streets.

Kath felt there needed to be a place to which people could be accepted back if they made a mistake. Her vision is of a number of small hostels that can be run as communities; in large hostels, people can just disappear. Originally a separate Trust, in the late 1990s it was amalgamated into St Martin-in-the-Fields Social Care Unit, and the hostel was converted into individual flats.

As we have seen, people without permanent housing are marginalised. They are viewed by society as "less than", "other", often with a severe effect on their self-esteem and thus their ability to overcome their problems. The Catholic Workers Movement, founded in the States during the Great Depression, has been highly influential, not only in the States, in its establishment of Houses of Hospitality. The founder, Dorothy Day, wrote:

The mystery of poverty is that by sharing in it, making ourselves poor in giving to others, we increase our knowledge and belief in love.

These are communities made up of those who embrace voluntary poverty in order to live alongside those whose poverty is not a choice. Simon Communities, based on this example, are one of the earliest instances of such a way of life in the UK.

Emmaus Communities also attempt to provide inclusive homes, in more than forty countries. There are fourteen in the UK, and more developing. They exist to enable people to move on from homelessness, providing work and a home in a supportive, family environment. Companions, as residents are known, give forty hours' work a week, collecting, renovating and reselling donated furniture in return for accommodation, food, clothing and a small weekly allowance. This work supports the community financially and enables residents to develop skills and rebuild their self-respect. Communities are suitable for those with low-support needs; no alcohol or drugs are allowed on the premises.

Emmaus is clear that once someone comes to live in their community, they are no longer homeless; they are "formerly homeless". Emmaus is a home. A former staff resident of an Emmaus community gave me a slightly different perspective. He found living there tough, and he worried about bullying and the amount of support given to Companions.

In May 08 I went to visit one of the newest communities, in South London. Open just for a few months, it was still building its community, both literally (they were waiting for a workshop and their own warehouse) and in terms of those who were living there. A core group had been established, and others will join it, at the rate of two a month, for however long they wish to stay – there are no restrictions on the length of time a resident stays. Residents might come from other communities, be referred by other agencies or self-refer.

They have a rented warehouse, two shops, an allotment where they are growing vegetables, and four staff, one of whom lives in. There is a flat for the community leader, not yet appointed. The main building is a former tram shed, a long thin building which has been renovated to a high standard with 25 rooms, all en-suite, and large bright communal rooms. Lunch is an important communal activity; we ate at a long table: Companions, volunteers and two French students who are both working there and paying for their keep. The patron of the organisation is Terry Waite, who happened to visiting there that day and sat next to me at lunch. He has been in at the beginning of the UK Emmaus, in 1992. The first community, in Cambridge, now has a turnover of £¼ million, and gives money to start other communities.

Elizabeth is a Companion Assistant, who helps with

administering the community. She is a local resident, who referred herself when her business took a downward path, and her landlady asked for a 40% rent increase. She couldn't afford to stay, or to move, and rang Emmaus in desperation. She had felt isolated, and is happy in community, finding the balance of privacy and company about right. Others have found it difficult: one left after four days, saying she was "a private person". Elizabeth says that she too is "private", but that boarding school was a good preparation for living with others. Community, she says, is something you have to work at.

Jim was working in one of the Emmaus shops round the corner when I spoke to him. He too manages the balance, but recognises that this way of life isn't for everyone. He came from a larger community in rural surroundings, so an urban home is quite a change, and he is still adjusting. Jim feels it is important to have goals. His plan is to move out when he feels ready, but, even though Emmaus has a detailed moving-on policy, independence – coping with rent and bills, and so on – is a big step.

The Big Issue Book of Home gives a snapshot of ideas about home both from homeless people and from people working in the homelessness sector, *and it does not distinguish between those who are homeless and those who are not.* That inclusion is crucial: our dreams are the same; psychological understanding can come from anyone. Running a mobile library for homeless people was another marker in my understanding of equality. Why should we assume that someone unfortunate enough to have lost a home is less intelligent, less educated, than we are? The reverse is often the case.

Mike gives a working definition of homelessness: "It is not having the right and security to stay where you are sleeping. A hostel will be a day ticket; if on a friend's floor or in temporary housing, it will be someone else's call." A woman refugee said, "Home is bound up with freedom; the knowledge that you can go back to the same place." A roofless man wrote:

My view on homelessness is that it is a state of mind. I meet many people in houses that are going through much more anguish than I am. They may be lonely, have mental health problems. Inside I am less homeless than a lot of people I meet (quote from Walker in the *Big Issue*).

4

The O of wheels

On the move

Apparently I'm homeless –

I find this quite amusing as I do in fact own my own home. I'm the only member of my family who can say this. I can't help but respect my eldest brother who will own his place in less than twenty years, and my sister and her new husband who are about to sign themselves up to a similar long term bondage agreement. My home may have cost a lot less but I'm still proud of it. I quite like the idea of having wheels on my home as well. When I get bored with the view I can go and find a better one...

Gary Brighton in Ephraums, 65

The nomadic way of life is an ancient one, though increasingly rare in industrialised societies. Until some ten thousand years ago, when mankind discovered the virtues of agriculture and domesticating animals, our hunter-gathering species was always on the move, in search of animals to kill or berries and fruits to pick, moving on according to the seasons or as pasture became exhausted. The constant need to move limited the possessions anybody could accumulate. Although diminishing in number, there are still some thirty to forty million pastoral nomads in the world, moving with their households in search of pasture for their animals.

Mongols, a hardy people, are traditionally nomadic, and 40% of the population still is. Life is linked to the land and to the animals, and several times a year families pack up and move on to better pasture, usually in groups of five to eight families. Wild and domesticated animals sometimes merge; Mongolia is a country of no private land.

Mongol homes are inviting, hospitable places, within a very traditional framework. All visitors are welcome. If the owners are away, visitors are expected to make themselves at home. In a climate of such extreme temperatures, shelter can be a matter of life and death. We stayed in the Gobi desert in a snow-bound spring, when night temperatures were -20°.

Gers [Mongols do not like the Soviet word, yurt] are large circular tents with a parasol structure, rising to a point in the middle, with a hole for the chimney of the central stove. The arrangement of gers is pretty standard. The master bed is at the back of the ger, others to right and left, with an altar area to the right of the main bed with shrine and candle and some precious possessions. If the owners are not Buddhist, the altar will consist mainly of family photos. The cooking and eating area (we sat on little stools) is in the centre; near the entrance is stored a container of precious water where people wash their hands and face, usually taking the water into the mouth and squirting it on to their hands to wash.

...There is no privacy inside the ger or out. Lavatorial activities take place round the back of the ger ... This is an outdoor culture, and a cold one.

...On arrival at a ger, the customary call is not of "hello" but "Nokhoi Khor" ("hold the dog"). Dogs are fierce here, sometimes rabid, and to be taken seriously. Once inside, we were always offered tea, made by heating a vast bowlful of water on the stove, a little milk and salt added, and a sprinkling of tea dust. We got quite used to this salty drink; any hot drink is welcome.

...Etiquette, as our guide book informed us, is complex. Don't step on the threshold, don't touch someone's hat, don't point your feet at anyone. Don't show your wrists, spill milk or write in red ink. On entering, walk clockwise round to the left, sitting towards the back in the area reserved for guests. Everything is given and received with both hands, or the right one, supported by the left. There are rituals surrounding the offering of snuff or vodka, even if the owner is too poor for the ornate bottle actually to contain anything. Never throw anything on the fire. Fire is sacred (Kavanagh, 2004: 169-70).

Most nomadic Mongols have no electricity but radios, horses and, increasingly, motor bikes to cross the huge distances. This is a sparsely populated country, but the fourth largest in the world.

"Peripatetic nomads" are mobile populations moving among settled populations and offering a craft or trade. The largest number of traditional peripatetic nomads are the Roma people, of whom there are an estimated 15 million world-wide: exact numbers are hard to gauge, as many Roma refuse to register their ethnic identity in official censuses because of a well-founded fear of discrimination. The largest Roma population is found in the Balkan peninsula, with significant numbers in the Americas, the former Soviet Union, Western Europe, the Middle East, and North Africa.

Peripatetic nomads in England are usually grouped under the term "Gypsies and Travellers", and may include travelling show people, those who were born on the road, who may or may not be of Romany descent, those who have taken to it recently – seeking homes, work or a change from city life – and those who travel seasonally. As George Monbiot wrote, "they are united by one inescapable fact: their mode of existence sets them apart from other people".

UK planning law defines Gypsies as people with a nomadic way of life. While this is historically true, it is a way of life threatened both by the disappearance of seasonal agricultural work, and by increasingly restrictive laws. New regulations both release local authorities from their duty to provide sites, and give police powers to remove caravans if there has been any damage to property, or if there are more than six caravans.

As a result, most Gypsies have now settled. According to the twice-yearly count by local authorities, in January 2006 there were over 15,500 Gypsy and Traveller caravans in England, some on private sites, a small number on unauthorised sites, and the majority on sites provided by local authorities. No numbers are available for those living in more permanent buildings.

It was with rather vague directions, and some nervousness, that I found my way to a Gypsy encampment in East London. I had not warned anyone of my visit, and was unsure of my welcome. But the gates to the spacious site stood wide open, and, although I got some curious looks, no one asked me my business. And, against expectation, it was all surprisingly familiar. A neat row of numbered bungalows in what might be called a street, behind railings over which numerous mats were hanging to air. Inside one of the buildings, Lisa and her sixteen-year-old daughter were in the middle of cleaning an already impeccably clean sitting room/kitchen. She agreed to speak to me, but remained standing, and cleaning, as we spoke. The room was bright and well if simply furnished, with a state-of-the-art television and a large plaster statue of the Virgin Mary.

Four of Lisa's five children live with her. They have been here since March 08, when they and six other families were moved, expensively and somewhat controversially, from an encampment near the London Olympic site. Lisa was born in Dublin, but came over with her parents when she was fourteen. Her parents had 17 children and moved around all their lives – her father working as a carpet-fitter – and she herself was on the road until about 16 years ago. She says she can't bear to live in houses. (The distinction is between living in this brick-built building and living in the general community.) Where she is now is near the caravans, there's room for the children to play out and she's surrounded by family. Three sisters and an aunt live near

53

by: in fact one of her sisters dropped in while I was there. Living in a settled way means that the children can get an education; Lisa and her sisters never learnt to read or write, but her daughter is now at college. She worries about the children being able to get accommodation like theirs, but at least they'll be educated and be able to get jobs. Lisa is not nostalgic about the nomadic way of life; living with her family and in community is what matters.

As a child, Paul lived for a while with a group of Gypsies in Oxford. It was a big community, of about 30 horse-drawn caravans, and the people lived by their wits, still, for instance, making the old-fashioned clothes pegs. "I think they found me useful, so they let me stay around. The caravans were very small – you could hear the snoring and smell things you'd rather not – but very beautiful."

But most of his childhood was spent with fairground people. He was, as he says, "adopted by the fairgrounds" at about the age of six. He'd never known his parents and had been brought up till then in homes and with foster carers. But he kept running away. He couldn't be kept away from the fairgrounds, fascinated by the rides, by the machinery and the smell of oil. He felt comfortable; he felt at home. He lived at one ground after another: no one could keep him – but he was, he says, a creative child, and wanted to learn. This was his way of life till he went to art school at the age of 17, and to some extent afterwards. All the fairgrounds are different, Paul says: it's a mistake to think all show people are the same: they're just as different from each other as other people. Sometimes a fairground will have men who have run away from their wives or the law; others are solid communities. Fairground people, he says, are good family people, very caring of children, and they look after each other in a very loving way. He stayed both at stationary fairgrounds – which were mainly seasonal, though there was a lot of maintenance work to be done off-season – and with ones that moved around.

Although some fairground people live in caravans, the traditional home is a wagon. The wagons are huge, very long, with two axles, and have to be drawn by a lorry. They are, Paul says, real family homes with rather 1930s interiors, a lot of wood, clean – and very private. Few outsiders are allowed inside.

Paul is sad that the old rides are going, and that beautifully hand-carved wood is giving way to manufactured fibre glass. Rides are becoming something for a quick thrill and to impress your mates. The clientele are getting younger too, as nine to twelve year olds have more spending power. But he doesn't feel that the way of life has changed at all, "thank goodness". Yes, he misses the life, but he goes back to visit – "you couldn't not." Paul is now in his fifties, although his elfin looks make him seem a lot younger. "I haven't had time to age," he says with a laugh. He is still creative, building old cars and boats, and writing poetry. He currently works as an accommodation officer in a student hostel, enjoying the comings and goings. "Home", he says, "is where I am. It's very rare I don't feel at home. The people fascinate me, make me laugh and cry."

Now, he says, he's no longer nomadic, but when I asked where he lives, he says that it varies. He has ten children from nine partners – and they are all current, so he spreads his time between them. A nomadic life of a different sort.

On the water

When I was growing up, I remember friends of my parents, probably then in their fifties or sixties (for me at that age they were simply "old"), who lived on a narrow boat. Their way of life seemed highly eccentric. Painters, vegetarians, they lived on one boat and exhibited on another. In the 1950s they were pioneers in a way of life that, although still unusual in industrialised societies, has become more popular.

"Jessie" is one of half a dozen narrow boats moored in a basin in London's East End opposite some giant Dutch barges, and in the midst of the tower blocks of the financial centre of Canary Wharf. It's a temporary mooring while work for the London Olympics is done near their usual mooring. The boat owners hope to be back by the end of 2008. Jessie is six foot wide and 62 feet long, divided into a sitting area, galley kitchen, bathroom (including a small bath), and bedroom. There are areas to sit out at front and back, a coal-burning stove in the sitting area, bottled gas for cooking and to power the fridge.

John and Rachel bought Jessie a couple of years ago, having rented a narrow boat in central London for a year to see how it felt. Neither of them had ever been on a narrow boat before but felt drawn to that way of life. Rachel had been living abroad, John with friends. They wanted to find somewhere together, and a boat seemed the answer. It wasn't to do with money, but about a different, simpler, way of life. Having seen an advertisement for a boat for rent, their first step was to Google "houseboat for rent in London", and their life on boats began.

They were particularly attracted to Jessie because she came complete with a mooring, something not always easy to find in London. They pay a regular fee for the mooring which comes with facilities such as free laundry, water, a pump out for their sewage tank, and an electrical connection. They also have 12 volt power charged by the boat's batteries, for when they are cruising. The day after I visited, they were going to have an inverter installed so that they could have a plug on the boat. It's a simple way of life. As John says, having supplies coming on in tangible "chunks" (coal, gas, water etc) makes them much more aware of what they consume.

Boats are not linked to the housing market and its fluctuations. They do not appreciate in the same way as houses but hold their value if looked after; maintenance needs to be more regular than for a house. As John says, if something needs to be done, it soon becomes obvious. Although living on a boat is seen as more vulnerable than living in a house, on a residential mooring such as this one there's a security gate to pass through. Most of all, living on a narrow boat is to be part of what is almost an extended family. It's a community of people of all ages and backgrounds who are committed to a particular way of life. The owners of the other boats are all friends – they eat together, borrow chairs, cutlery etc. if they have guests, light a neighbour's stove so that the boat will be warm on return from a few days away. Rachel and John share an internet connection with one of their neighbours.

Rachel says it's an outdoorsy way of life. Hatches can be opened right up to the sky, so that passers by can poke their heads in! They have a direct interaction with their neighbours which would be impossible if they lived in a flat or house. They cruise about half a dozen times a year, but trips have to be carefully timed according to the tides, and they usually have to wait until there are enough boats to make it worth opening the large lock on to the Thames River. A weekend trip can take a fortnight.

Both cycle to work, and they have a tandem for joint outings. They don't go out much in the evenings, particularly in the winter: the cosiness of the stove is too appealing. Floating on water deadens sound coming in or going out so even in the heart of London it's very quiet, especially on their old mooring, where you can hear the ducks swim by. Neither can imagine any other way of life. Rachel says that there is nothing in the boat that she would be devastated to lose – books, papers, clothes, nothing. Except the boat itself. "Jessie", she says, "is a person."

No fixed abode

A few years ago I sold my London home. It was a pretty flat with a little private garden and a large sitting room in a much sought-after area, across the road from Hampstead Heath, twenty minutes from central London. But it was not, though, a flat that ever felt close to my heart. When I went travelling for a year I found that living out of a rucksack, staying among those with very little, distanced me from the need for many of my possessions and, it seemed, from the need for a permanent "home". It was a strange discovery. Home is such a central part of our "normal" life in the West, and I suppose in most parts of the world. But now that I was alone and did not need to feather a nest for anyone else, the geography of my existence did not seem to be central.

I knew it was likely to be a temporary state but in the meantime was interested to explore the prospect of deliberate homelessness. I knew the restrictions that truly homeless people live with – hard to access a doctor, a dentist, library; excluded from so much that we take for granted – and knew that I was a privileged person: I could give my mother's house for an address if necessary, and I needed in any case to spend a few days there every month. I was able to make choices.

Not that I was consciously deciding to take this course; it seemed to have grown out of a "not knowing" that I had to obey. The process was becoming a familiar one. Five years before, I had let go of my business, my work of some 25 years, without any sense of what I was to do. It led to a complete change in my life. The process of letting go was a startling discovery of a freedom that I vowed would shape the rest of my life. This was the next step.

So I gave my children much of the furniture they grew up with, and a lump sum to help them on the housing ladder. I put everything that I could either on-line or on direct debit; and put my stuff in storage until I knew that I would not want it. One step at a time. Although I was hitting the road at the time of life that a Hindu becomes a *sannyasi*, I was not planning to give everything away or become dependent on others. I admired, even envied, the rooted life, but just knew that that was not to be for me, at least for the time being.

"If everything in your house has a story," writes Jeanette Winterson, "it's a home." Yes, and that's precisely what I find, somewhat to my surprise, that I have let go of. I don't want constant reminders of other people, other times. Not that they were unhappy, or that they provoke a sense of loss of happier times, but simply that I want to concentrate on the present, not be distracted. I don't need objects to remind me of people I love. The nomadic impulse now seems to have stilled for a while, but I still don't feel the need of a geographic home. It simply doesn't matter where I am. If that means staying put for a while, that's fine too.

Jo has also chosen to be nomadic, but on a smaller income she has fewer choices. She had been her mother's carer for several years, before her mother's death and her own eviction. "If I weren't the person I am, prepared to treat it as an adventure, I could be on the streets, could have committed suicide." She writes:

Recently I became of no fixed abode. It was a conscious decision, though one I would rather not have had to make, but financial constraints meant I had little choice. It's very scary, getting to sixty and finding oneself without a roof over one's head, but rather than panic, I chose to see it as an opportunity. I found a very part-time live-in job for six months in France, then I just wandered, mainly in France, for the next six months...

Recently I have been staying with friends in Britain. At the moment I am staying in a community – a very bohemian household. Having lived alone for a very long time, I'm out of the habit of considering other people. The upside is I'm making a lot of really nice friends. The downside is I wish I could have my own space. I live out of my car and though there have been times when I have taken a siesta in my car, I have not yet had to sleep overnight in it. Amazingly, my cost of living is greatly reduced, so much so that if I did find myself without a bed for the night I could book into a B&B. This is not a long-term solution but for the moment I am living in the moment.

"The biggest challenge to this way of living simply", she says, "is the system." Without an address her car insurance becomes invalid, she cannot vote and will have difficulty in accessing medical care or any kind of insurance. Even a post office box needs a residential address.

> Without my car I would find it impossible to carry with me the things I still feel I need about me. It's amazing how little I do need but my needs still fill my small car. I carry with me some "essentials", such as bedding, my laptop...my sewing machine... my electric screwdriver and an apron. With these I find I can survive... I only need about a week's clothes to keep me going. Plus, of course, a woolly and a waterproof, wellies and walking boots. A smallish suitcase and a similar size bag carry the clothes. There is a suitcase of winter clothes stashed with a friend...
>
> I appreciate that this lifestyle is not for everyone and I am very aware that I cannot maintain it for many years as signs of arthritis and the like are already manifesting themselves...I can't afford to buy a house that is habitable and I know I do not want to live completely alone. I do know of a property for sale which could make three or four housing units... It would be an ideal place to set up a small community...
>
> I love the life I am living. All my friends tell me I am more relaxed and less loud than I was. I'm much more confident in myself. For now it suits me, despite the challenges posed (the *Friend*, 29 August 2008, and conversation 6 October 2008).

Valerie is in her fifties and comes from a big farming family. She does not have a home of her own but is very much part of the rural community in which she lives. She rented a house locally for a while but found it cost too much. She makes a living from gardening, cleaning, and odd jobs, but refuses to take money for house-sitting, or caring for animals where necessary. She moves around the country neighbourhood in which she lives, wherever a room is available. She is well known in the area, and there's always somewhere for her to go. "No one", said a neighbour, "could control Valerie in any way. She's a free spirit."

John T writes: "People often say to me I must be mad to live a nomadic lifestyle by choice. It set me thinking just what are the advantages to this way of life so I started to list them." This list includes "waking up in the morning to the birds' dawn chorus" and "badgers playing with cubs in the moonlight". The downside, he finds, is the wholesale destruction of all kinds of animals and birds on the roads, in the quest for more speed.

"So", he writes, "I've got news for you. I'd rather be mad in my home than sane in yours" (Ephraums, 21).

5

The O of safety

Home is where the heart is

Home is a pair of open arms
Home is a peg on which you hang
Your paintings, woes and trousers up
An escape from harm, a warm
Retuner to brave the twangs
A face-lift or a chin-up.

A sculpted self of colour choice
The whispered word of décor voice
A cushion here, a carpet there
The print of me outstretched to share

The "How was your day, dear?
Do pull up a chair here"
To laugh or cry or scream or clown
"Just turn that bloody music down"

The faces and sounds of where I belong
Explode inside like a fart or a song
The pigeons and tits
The cooing and shits

Flowers, scent, the fragrance lent
The soft caress and tenderness
Of grass and hedge, petal or veg
Symbols all of my four walls.

Gill Lowther, 2008

The attic was a lovely place to play. The large, round, coloured pumpkins made beautiful chairs and tables. The red peppers and the onions dangled overhead. The hams and the venison hung in their paper wrappings, and all the bunches of dried herbs, the spicy herbs for cooking and the bitter herbs for medicine, gave the place a dusty-spicy smell.

Often the wind howled outside with a cold and lonesome sound. But in the attic Laura and Mary played house with the squashes and pumpkins, and everything was snug and cosy (Laura Ingalls Wilder, *Little House in the Big Woods*, Methuen, 2000, 10-11).

"Snug and cosy": like many images in children's literature, the little house is a perfect picture of warm and secure family life that withstands the dangers of the outside world: the big woods, the howling wind, the bears. This is a dream of home that is a physical and emotional shelter. Wholesome, full of smells of home-made food, lovingly made with home-grown vegetables. A place that both symbolises and encompasses the activities and relationships that stand for home.

Fay is an architect who specialises in working with people to enable them to live "better" in the spaces that they have. To do so, she finds she needs to work hard on her understanding of people. She needs to find out who really makes the decisions and, like a doctor, she learns a great deal about her clients that she cannot discuss outside, and needs to forget when the job is finished. "Bathrooms!" she said. "What you can learn about people from their bathrooms!"

Before working with anyone, Fay asks: "What are all the things that you don't need?

"What do you really love?

"What do you hate?"

Some people find her questioning intrusive but, she says, it is the only way to understand what people really want. They often don't know themselves why they have asked her in; usually it is because there is a problem, often with their own relationships. And sometimes clients don't need any work done, just to make the most of unused spaces – most people, she says, have parts of their houses that are barely used, or are stuck with choices made years before, like "that sofa has always been there".

One young couple I spoke to said, "our home may not be one for the ideal home show but it makes up for it with a lot of love inside. A home isn't about appearance; it's about the energy and moments the place soaks up and radiates out, that determines whether we feel comfortable inside it..."

"I hate going home."

No, not the cry of a woman suffering domestic abuse, nor a teenager longing to fly the nest, but a married woman with three grown-up children coming back from holiday. "My house here is very comfortable," she says slowly. "But it's dangerous territory for me. I don't really want to go there. It's not really a place of safety. I've always dreaded coming home." Her unhappiness has nothing to do with her current family life, nor the comfortable house in an area that she loves; it has everything to do with her experience of an unloving childhood, a time when she used to delay her return from school, from anywhere. Even now, when she returns from holiday she hides away for a day or two before re-emerging into the world. Her anger about "home", she says, stems from a time in her early twenties when, unable to take any more, she walked out of her parental home, taking with her a few belongings in a suitcase, to sleep on a friend's floor. Weeks later, having found a flat, she recalled her father's birthday, and rang him. After a short silence she heard, "When you leave like that, it's a one-way ticket. You don't come back."

The womb is our first home, where all our needs are met: warm, fed, nurtured, utterly secure. Leaving it is a shock, often a traumatic one. For most people their concept of home is formed in childhood: if they are lucky, a warm, safe, nurturing environment in which to develop, surrounded by the love of parents and other family. One woman, who as a child lived in London during the Second World War, said that emotional support was more important than physical security. "Even when we had bombing, it was still home." Sadly, the experience for many is far from that place of emotional safety. Whatever the experience, it remains a reference point throughout life.

When I ask around what the word "home" means to people, talk is rarely of a present home. Even middle-aged people with grown families and beautiful and cared-for houses, refer to childhood – and many of the responses reveal a considerable degree of insecurity and pain. Early experiences, well hidden in apparently well-adjusted and established people, erupt. Janet spoke of a home where good meals were eaten round the family table; good conversation circulated. But, she said, "the first image that comes to me at the thought of home is that there was no seat for me at the table."

Paul, who is in the process of divorce, says,

Home? I'm hugely ambivalent about that word. It means "haven" to me but it also means that it ought to be a haven and might be disappointing [he nearly said "tainted"]. I have a tendency to turn houses into little prisons if I'm not careful. Obviously it's also the four walls that you know, but there's a danger. It's to do with an unhappy home in childhood, and my marriage, which wasn't what it seemed. I associate it with something that isn't what it seems from the outside. At the same time I get jumpy when I don't have one.

Rose, who has chosen to leave behind her flat and career to start a new life as a spiritual counsellor, has nothing to go to in a few months' time, when her course finishes. "I'm terrified," she said. "It's absolutely primal." She remembers, as a child, standing with her mother and boxes on the pavement, wondering whether the social worker would find them somewhere to live.

Childhood insecurity is closer to the surface than we realise. Some years ago, when the building trade was foundering, and a lot of architects lost their jobs, my boyfriend couldn't afford to pay the mortgage. His flat was repossessed. It was a shocking experience but we were not living together, so my terror was ostensibly out of all proportion. It was only later that I made the connection. As a child, when my father fell ill, there was a question for some time as to whether we would have to leave our house. In the end his employer paid off the mortgage, but, underground, the childhood fear had remained.

For John, home is "almost everything. Being safe, being together with each other, being able to welcome people." He then says tellingly, "I didn't know how to use a house when I was a lad." A pause, then:

> People make bad choices. My aunt had a shop. We moved in with her, expecting to take it over. Then relations broke down. One sister went to stay with another aunt who was not on speaking terms, and my sister wasn't allowed back. When we had our own place I didn't know what to do in a house when there's no one to tell you not to do things. Still, now, my wife has all the running of the house. Maybe that's left over from then.

"What does 'home' mean to you?"

From the dozens of people I have asked this question, often the first reaction is "a place to call my own", "privacy", "my own space", "safety", "security", The outside world, it seems, is not a friendly place; being out in the world is a challenge.

Jane runs a busy café with her husband. Long hours on her feet, making sandwiches on demand, mostly to a regular clientele, with a welcoming smile and chat. Despite being in the middle of London, with thousands of workers travelling in and out each day, it feels like a community café. For Jane, home is a place to relax after the tensions of the day, somewhere to retreat to, to "feel safe, comfortable and cosy. Somewhere where you can shut the door and forget about everyone outside. Peace and quiet. I'm a bit anti-social, really," she says with an embarrassed grin.

Even more, perhaps, home is somewhere to drop defences, the public face, free from the need to make an impression; it is somewhere with the freedom to "be oneself".

Alex is a barrister in her thirties. For her, home is somewhere you can come back to knowing that all your things will be there, comfortable and secure, where you can be alone if you want to, have the music you want, the TV. Freedom. Having lived with strangers, she feels a lot freer sharing a flat with a good friend.

For Margot, who lives alone in London, home is about privacy. "No one comes through that door unless I say so." At the same time, she seemed unperturbed by an intruder who came through the open ground-floor window into her bedroom at night. When I asked why she didn't lock it, she said she'd rather have an intruder than to have to lock herself in. "I definitely want to control who enters my home and not, but I'm not prepared to use much 'force' to *avert* the wrong entry. I don't invite Jehovah's Witnesses in and I experience telephone sales calls as strongly intrusive. I am told I can be intimidating despite my size and I would use intimidation without misgiving to oust the wrong person."

When I asked Grazyna about "home", she was surprised to find that security "came up" very strongly. "Peace, protection, a quiet place." Born in this country of Polish and Italian parents, she is a charity worker who travels throughout Africa for most of the year, often spending just a couple of weeks in the UK before going away again. Her most recent trips have been to Pakistan just as a state of emergency was announced, leaving a few weeks before some members of the staff she was working with were killed, and Dafur.

I have always considered Chris a pacifist: when he was punched on the nose by a young man stealing his sister's purse, he didn't retaliate. However, when talking about houses, he said that if someone broke in, he'd want to shoot him. When I reminded him of his former pacific response, he said: "That was just a punch on the nose; this is my home."

Family

Man wanted a home, a place of warmth, or comfort, first of physical warmth, then the warmth of the affections.
Thoreau, 17

What parents can offer is a home, a place that is receptive but also has the safe boundaries within which their children can develop and discover what is helpful and what is harmful... to develop the freedom that gives them the courage to leave the home and travel. The hospitable home indeed is the place where father, mother and children can... support each other in their common struggles to live and to make live (Nouwen, 57).

We used to go to school with torn clothes and shoes, but we never laughed at each other because... that's just the way it was. I didn't have anything but I was happy. I could feel the love within our home. Everyday when I came home from school I could feel the love we had for one another. The way your parents raise you, how much love they give you, you feel this within yourself and when they hold you, you can feel the warmth and the love from their bodies. When you're taken away from that it's very hard (a Chiricahua Apache elder in Chapman, 26).

It's strange how clear the house of my grandparents remains.

They lived by the sea, on the south coast of England, and most holidays I would go and stay with them. The regular routine of their lives was reassuring, a constant in uncertain times. Every day my grandfather would take a cold shower, cut out *The Times* crossword, and throughout the day we would ponder one clue or another. In the morning, winter or summer, towel rolled up under his arm, he would walk down to the beach and bathe; when I was staying there, I went with him. Lunch was at one, supper at 7pm. At 6pm my grandfather would wind up the clocks in the house; before supper was sherry; after supper, cubes of dark chocolate. And if he had not finished the crossword, my grandfather would take it up to bed to think about the last couple of clues.

The house was full of objects from their travels, especially their years in Peru where, astonishingly, my grandfather was postmaster general; and of lovely portraits of my grandmother in her opera-singing years. I remember where things were in that house far more than objects in my own houses.

Fay too has a clear memory of her grandparents' home by the sea, but in her case it was her home too for the first seven years of her life before she was whisked off to live with her father in strange and more affluent places. It was a simple life in Ghana, with a clear routine: of sweeping the sandy courtyard early before school, and before the sand got too hot for bare feet; of fetching water. Fay remembers in detail the scale and proportion of the rooms; only the bedrooms, she said, had roofs.

For Karl, his grandparents' house, just up the street from his own, was a refuge from the noise of siblings, animals and television. A quiet ordered place to do homework and have a conversation.

Rose can't bear the thought of the selling of her grandmother's house, a house she has always known. "If I'd lived there I would have hated it. It's because it was a refuge. I'd knock on the door and she'd always be in and make me a cup of tea – that's what Nans are. When she goes there'll be nothing."

Familiarity, routine, regularity can be very comforting for a child – and memorable. And as Virginia, who spent the first five years of her life in South Africa, said: "Your earliest years have the most powerful effect on you of any in your life. Patterns are so deeply embedded." She quoted the old Jesuit saying: "Give me a child until he is seven and I will give you the man."

Susan grew up in London in the 1960s. She now lives with her husband, David, and four daughters in a large Georgian house not very far from where she lived as a child. It was an interesting time to ask her about home: only David was currently living in the building, as the whole place was being converted into flats: the rest of the family were staying with friends and family. Both she and David write and work from home. "It's the most important place for me, though it isn't that much about security," she says. "Family is so important. I'm pretty adaptable, but I like having the sense that it is a place for the family to come back to. Normality, relaxation, an oasis.

"It was so even when I was a kid, though the place was rubbish. It was a poor background: rented rooms in a big house. It was Dickensian, black brick, in a square." Both sets of grandparents lived in the same square, as did an aunt and a great aunt. There were three such families with different branches living in that square – "a strong sense of community". The four children played out: "The square was our little world." Her father was a plasterer, self-employed, so got no help from the State; her mother did two cleaning jobs. There was no money or car; no washing machine or fridge, and no bathroom. Washing dishes, clothes and bodies took place in the sinks and in a tin bath in the kitchen; a washing line across the kitchen, a mangle in the garden. For two years, she remembers, there was no lighting upstairs. Susan reflects that she has never had her own bedroom. As a child she shared first with her parents and brother, then with her sister; as an adult, she has always shared with her husband. "Not unusual," she says. All the children were born at home. "No one owned a place. It was part of the consciousness. If you were in a place owned by the council, you were doing well."

The family moved out in 1971-2 when a compulsory purchase order was made on the square, and they were offered a flat on the estate where her sister still lives. Her Gran, who was given the flat above them, was keen to move as she had never had a bathroom and, living on the second floor, she had to go down to the ground floor to the loo. Even after Susan had her own house, if she dreamt of a building, she would dream of the house in which she grew up.

Margaret, who works in Kolkata, India, describes a typical home to which she went to do a dyslexia test. It's down an alley too narrow to get a zimmer frame. Seven people live in one room, the four women on the bed; three men on mats on the floor. Every corner is stuffed with papers; the bed is high so that belongings can be kept underneath. The kitchen is in the room; a little space beyond is "the room we pray in". When asked about a fan, they pointed to the hole in the ceiling. From this room, one daughter trained to be a Montessori teacher; one of the sons is studying to be an accountant, and another daughter went to Edinburgh University to gain an MBA. Every time the father shows a picture of his daughter receiving her degree, complete with gown and mortar board, he cries. Despite an electric shut-down for two hours every night, all the studying has been done in that room.

Before her own marriage broke up, Margaret, her husband and four children had a large house with "good-sized rooms, where everyone had their own space". Togetherness with their friends. "If it isn't spatially, visually done with tenderness and care," she says, "those aspects of your personality shrink." When her marriage was teetering on the edge, she said that her greatest concern was the break-up of the home.

When the home no longer exists because the babies have gone or the home is broken up through lack of finances, etc, your foundations are rocked. But the responsibility to keep the home going just in case the now grown-up babies need it – the place where memorabilia can be lodged and retrieved when needed – familiar stuff around is security even when babies are long gone, Oh I didn't know you had kept that sort of thing. So to lose a home – I was completely devastated, and I suppose I have tried ever since to set up a home of sorts again where we can gather. It's an anchor for the family. It overwhelms me sometimes when they come here [her studio flat in London]. It makes me unhappy that I can't give them something better. Knowing how my mother had a grand home.

Since retirement she spends the bulk of the year working in India, but says: "I would never call my flat in Kolkata home." Her family is in England.

Unlike Margaret, I have given up the role of guardian of the memorabilia. My mother's house, the house I grew up in, is full of familiar objects and full of her presence; my children are building their homes. I have given most of the memorabilia to them. I am the generation that is skipping the need for a family home; it seems to me that there are enough of them to keep the family going.

For most of the people I talked to, home is about being with the people they love. A place where you can always go back and be accepted for who you are. Acceptance, love, being valued for yourself. For Frankie, anywhere she is staying with her family becomes home. When her children were smaller she and her family holidayed together with her twin sister and family on the Scilly Isles. She remembers those idyllic times and saying to one of the children, "Come on, let's go home."

"Home?" said the child, perplexed, "but that's in Marlow."

"No, I mean the cottage here."

"Home", Frankie said, "is wherever we are together."

Four-year old Titus felt that living with strangers in his house would not be home, but that being with his parents somewhere else would. Family is all.

Despite having grown children of her own, Anne's home is always "where Mum and Dad are". And for Cliff it's simple: home is where his wife is.

Times of life

Teenage years bring a wish to separate, to move on, to leave home, to make one's own way in the world, perhaps to reject parental values. Home may even be seen as a trap, a prison, a place in which one is treated as a child, not allowed to grow into an independent being, although many young people come back to their parents' house for a time and young women in particular talk of going "home" when they are visiting their parents for the weekend.

After a period of independence, there is a pressure to settle, maybe with a partner, have children, nest. As Margaret, now a grandmother, said, "Having babies, bringing them into a home and all that getting ready and preparing".

A friend told me about the first intimation of his son's transition. Chris and his partner have been living a carefree, hedonistic life in Australia: partying, making the most of the outdoor culture. They have recently bought their first house. "Well," said Mike, as they chatted on the phone, "what will you be up to this weekend?"

"Oh, I think we'll have a quiet time. I've noticed a patch of damp that needs dealing with."

Olly is nesting too. Engaged to be married, in the first flat he has owned, he enjoys "wrapping himself up" in "an intermediary layer" of possessions, symbols and space. It's a buffer around him. His parents' home too is still home to him, since they live in the house in which he was born, and his experience in it has obviously influenced the way he wishes to live now. A garden was an important part of his life as a child, as his own is now: both are buffers, he says: between self and the wildness of nature.

In the Hindu culture, four stages of life are recognised. After a period of training of mind and body, the devout Hindu is expected to have a householder period; then, at about the age of 50, comes the period of *Vanprastha*: a retreat from the world, perhaps with a partner, handing over responsibilities to children. Finally there is a time to let go and work towards becoming a liberated soul and the mystic union with the Divine. In Western cultures a similar pattern may emerge. After a period of education and training in youth, there is often a period of career busyness, building a family and a home, before a possible stage of retreat, increased interiority and simplification of life. In secular terms, growing up, nesting, downsizing.

It is this later period with which many in the West find problems. Having built a career, with maybe a family growing up, there is often a period of stagnation and lack of purpose and, so far from downsizing, many use their increasing affluence to acquire more and more, filling the house with more expensive accessories, changing decoration or furniture according to the current fashion, finding in burnishing the surface of their lives that they are somehow making up for a sense of emptiness.

Empty nest

The moment of birth is the first step of a child away from the mother; growing up is a continuation of that process. It's a natural process, but not always one that is easy to adjust to. It is noticeable that in many Western cultures, children are staying longer at home, unwilling or financially unable to leave the nest. Some can't wait to go. And some parents can't wait to go either. I have heard several stories of parents who, when their children are at university, or even still at school, sell the house and move abroad, leaving their children to stay with friends, or to their own devices. Children may not be ready: it is easy to underestimate the power of a family home, and the long-term impact of what can feel like desertion.

Although for parents it brings with it a new freedom, the emptying of the nest can also feel like desolation. I felt the intimations when my younger child went to school: even more when they were both at university. I remember closing the door of our family home when they left, and weeping. Suddenly they were off, gone, the nest empty – and it wasn't helped by the fact that my husband had gone too. A home on your own may be fine, but it's harder when it is a home bereft of previous inhabitants; it can become a home with ghostly presence.

Living alone
What is a home if you do not share it with anyone?

After a conflictual relationship with a partner, or sharing with a flat-mate whose ways are not ours, to close the door behind them can be a relief; solitude a blessing. After all, it is a chance to exert absolute control over our surroundings. We can be messy or tidy, have quiet or noise (depending on the neighbours). Our own kind of music; put things where we want them and know they will not be moved; be sociable or solitary; sleep without interruption; not have to put up with other people's friends or tiresome habits, or have them criticise ours.

I have lived with others for most of my life. I lived with my parents until I was 21, was married from the age of 22 to 40; my children continued to live with me for another eight years. I then lived with a partner for five years, and one of the reasons I decided to dispense with a home was the break-up of that relationship. Although I enjoy my own company, if I am not making a home with someone, it doesn't matter where I am. For me, home is not about geography. Where I dwell does not have to be permanent, or belong to me.

Others think differently. Sara is single, a professional, with a beautiful house, full of modern art. For her, home is "where I'm at my most secure; it's my own private space." For Jo, a woman separated from her husband for some six years, her London flat is "almost a sacred space".

Frances, recently widowed and with grown-up children, said that for her: "home is where I'm safe and with the people I love (although I do not now live with those I love)." Even after they have left, the physical space represents their presence.

My mother, now 93, has lived in the same house for 54 years. Once a spacious suburban family home, it is now much too big for her but, since her sight is declining, it makes sense to stay in a space that she knows so intimately. It is precious, too: full of memories of the family; of the objects that remind her of them, of friends who have gone and of the many places she has been. It is also a place of hospitality: she still welcomes people to stay, or to come for meals. Visitors are frequent.

Jeannette Winterson writes of creating a happy home, even if you yourself are unhappy. "I believe that you have to begin with one single thing that you call your own... Private magic is about investing ordinary objects with talismanic power...Gradually if you have one safe calm space, the bigger space around you becomes safe and calm too" (Smolan and Erwitt, quoted in the *Independent*, 7 June 2008).

Homemaking and hospitality

Be a home
where love is
at home
Len Ball in Ephraums, 12

Maggie is at last content. After a busy professional life, bringing up a family, it took time to adjust to being at home. But now, that

is what she loves. "It's domesticity that makes me happy –
pottering around and making things as nice as they can be on a
limited budget. I just love home-making and cooking. While I
was working I didn't have the time to do it properly." And now,
indeed, she and her husband do it properly: in a simple, spare,
elegant house, with crisp white linen on the beds, few knick-
knacks, everything cared for, looked after. A caring, loving
stewardship of the environment in which they live.

Jo and Richard's London flat is a place of wonder: filled to the
rafters with objects, scarcely an inch of wall to be seen in the
spacious three-bedroom flat. In the kitchen stands a splendid
bulbous fridge bought by Richard's mother in 1952; opposite the
front door a battered nineteenth-century harmonium (covered in
dust, insists Jo), photos, postcards, little bits and pieces and "big
things I haven't got room for anywhere else. Plus things people
have sent me or I've picked up." In the centre, on a large piece of
cardboard, is the face of a beautiful Edwardian woman looking
straight at us, with big blue eyes and a look of lovely serenity on
her face. Above it is a family painting of a three-masted sailing
ship ("there were three of them so we each got one. We like this
one because it's got people on it"). Above that, high up on the
wall, is a plastic kite from Malaysia. To the side, a beautiful
portrait of Shakespeare painted on – an ashtray. A characteristic
combination of beauty and ephemera.

Richard says: "My ideas of home are very much inherited.
You only have to look around you to see how the past has
influenced me. I find I'm happy in the same places that my father
was happy as a schoolboy. Home is an extension of "house" to
the particular houses I was in with my family. Beyond that,
places where I have loyalty. In my case Cornwall above all else."

We have all known other people's houses in which we feel at
home. The ability to relax, to wander about, even to fall asleep in
front of the fire, in a place of love and security, an expression of
the character of their owners. It has nothing to do with wealth;

everything to do with love and generosity. When my partner and I travelled for a year, we joined a peacemaking organisation called Servas, in which people host travellers for a couple of nights in their own homes. On one occasion, in Costa Rica, we stayed with a couple in their self-built house with corrugated iron roof, sharing the main bedroom with them and their dog. Such generosity and open-heartedness towards strangers.

Frances is a homemaker *par excellence*. Always full of one project or another, she commits herself lovingly to an aspect of her home. The result is a place of warmth and welcome, felt as soon as one crosses the threshold. She extends loving hospitality, acceptance and friendship from a place of serenity and peace: an extension of her authentic self.

Hospitality is a sacred duty in many cultures: the stranger an honoured guest. Even in the security-conscious West, unquestioning hospitality is more common than we imagine, particularly when children grow up and leave home. Jim and Dorothy are an elderly couple living in the West Country. After their six children left home, they felt that they rattled in their big house. So they opened their doors – literally, since they never lock them – to homeless men and women, people seeking asylum or leaving prison. Now in their seventies, they get cards from their former guests, saying "Remember me?", and updating them with their news. Sharing a home with others is a richness for both parties.

For Lynn, home is somewhere she can welcome people to. Her parents, very politically involved, held an almost open house. Her mother took in people in trouble: once a family of four children whose mother was ill. Two came to live with the family; Lynn's mother offered to take the other two if necessary, and become the children's legal guardian. On another occasion, her mother brought home a homeless man off the street.

Ron wrote of a similar childhood experience. His father was a vicar and "there were always strangers and wayfarers coming to the vicarage: we fed them sandwiches and I would listen to their stories. I enjoyed the sense of offering hospitality." Ron went on to become the leader of Pilsden, an inclusive Christian community that welcomes people with mental health issues. "At Pilsden we each instinctively welcome the visitor – a welcome created with dignity, because we have all been welcomed here by others" (*Marshwood Vale* magazine, June 2008).

Meg's parents' house is always full, even though they are both in their seventies. She feels that if she and her new husband buy a big house, they will use it generously. "The only justification for a big house is to let anyone use it. You can't close the door."

For some, taking in lodgers is a way of life, as well as a necessary source of income. In her previous house, Gill had three or four lodgers at a time, in her smaller new one, probably one or two. They come from all round the world, keep in touch and often return. In the twenty-four years she has been doing this, she reckons that she has hosted 35 different nationalities. "They are part of my family," she says. "They regard me as an auntie or older sister. This is their London home." Gill has created an international community within the confines of her own home.

Giving is natural and necessary to human beings. One of the blights of homelessness is not to have a place to welcome others, a place from which one can proffer friendship. To stay in a place from which one has to be absent during daylight hours; a place in which there is no space for a private conversation; a place from which, with little warning, one might be ejected, is not to be at home.

Old age

Old age is unpredictable. We do not know how our health will be, or when and how we will die. There are often difficult decisions to be made about living safely with declining health. Sometimes people can live and die in their own homes, in a benison of continuity and security. Moving into sheltered accommodation is sometimes an option: sometimes a relief, sometimes a sadness at giving up much that is precious. Going – or worse, being put – into a home is an event dreaded by most elderly people: giving up all that has meant home to them over past years; most of their personal possessions, all the personal history, and, most of all, their independence.

My great-grandmother lived with my grandparents; she had her own room which she rarely left, taking all meals alone in that room. When my grandfather died, my grandmother sold her home and split her time between her two sons, my father and my uncle, living in each household as one of the family. My mother lives alone; we have never discussed living together, and I do not have expectations of living with either of my children when I am old. Times change. People rarely plan for their old age, just because it is so uncertain, and always seems a long way off. We react to circumstances as we find them. A decade or so ago I remember discussions with various women friends about buying a house together and living together in old age, perhaps with a nurse on site: looking after ourselves and each other. But we haven't done it. We are not old enough, or sure enough about how our lives will be in the indeterminate future.

Audrey, in her eighties, leads an independent life in the house she has lived in for 22 years, and shared with her husband until he died. It's just outside a seaside town in England, and the daily walk up a steep hill keeps her heart in good shape. When she becomes unable to climb up to her house, she will retreat to the old people's home a couple of miles away. She is on the long list. Each January they contact her to ask if she still wants to be on it. "Yes, but I'm not ready yet." Plans in place. A well-organised life.

Some enjoy the security and regular meals of an old peoples' home, being fussed over – maybe not an experience they have had in the recent past. But one woman, interviewed on radio, said: "It's very nice. It's not like home, naturally."

Trish's sister has recently gone into a home. Trish notes the shrinking of her sister's life; the institutionalisation that quickly sets in when you hand over almost every aspect of your personal care to others. It is a good place; people are kindly treated, but health and safety precautions place constraints on the residents, who are not allowed electric kettles in their rooms, or to take a bath without someone else present. Small invasions of precious privacy. "It's a micro-world," says Trish. "That's your place. Your confidence, your mind, your world shrink."

That sense of another world was apparent on visits to my father in his last months in a nursing home. When I crossed the threshold, it seemed to me that I was entering a parallel universe where behaviour obeyed no rules that were familiar to me, but the staff took it all in their stride. It was not an unhappy place. Indeed, the care that was given to my father was beautiful to behold. The matron said, "This place is about love," and so it was. The compassion of the (mostly young and low-paid) staff was demonstrated in their treatment of the old and demented, with humour, love and seemingly unending patience. And when my father was dying, they rang my mother so that we were able to spend his last night in his room and be with him when he died. It was all that we could have wished for.

But in the search for the right home, we had seen others where old people were lined up against the walls in chairs or wheelchairs, left all day in one room, with the television blaring; no activities, no bell in the lounge to ring for help; "homes" with sticky floors, an overpowering stench of urine, and sharp words for any "trouble" caused. Jean, who went into a care home briefly, said that if she had to stay there for the rest of her life it would have been "a slow death", and that policy makers needed to have "a greater vision of what it's like to be completely helpless". In our rapidly ageing populations – in the UK, it is estimated that the number of people over 85 will double in the next 25 years – the care of the elderly is a growing social and political priority. There are currently 12,000 care homes for the elderly in the UK, with nearly half a million beds, some excellent, many acceptable and some below an acceptable standard. In some, people with dementia are treated with psychotic drugs; in some, physical or emotional abuse takes place. Residents and relations are often frightened to complain: they don't want to rock the boat; are afraid of the consequences if they do.

Jean spoke of a woman who kept calling out, unanswered. When she mentioned it to staff, they said, "Take no notice, she's just old." Most of us will become old; what will our homes be? However difficult we may become, we still need the freedom to be who we are.

Death

The decision about where to be buried, or where to have ashes scattered is often a telling one. Jo and Richard are in their sixties, and have lived all their married lives in two places: a spacious flat in a purpose-built Edwardian block in London overlooking Hampstead Heath, and a cottage in North Cornwall. Both have strong Cornish roots. Discussing where they would like to be buried, Richard was clear that he wanted to be buried in Cornwall, not near their cottage but where his parents were buried – in North Cornwall. Jo also wants to be buried where her formative years were spent – in South Cornwall. "But", says Richard, "I want to be with you." They have agreed that whoever goes first will get to choose; the other will follow. Home is where the heart is, even in the grave.

My mother wants to have her ashes placed in the crematorium where my father's ashes are, and where most of her oldest friends have been laid to rest. I don't feel the placing of my dead body will be of importance but I have an inclination to be buried in a Quaker burial ground; in our meeting we have the right to be buried in Jordan's, an old burial ground in Buckinghamshire. It is not to do with personal connection, but in the context of my faith, the belonging that has to do with common values: equality, small headstones, plain names. Most of all I want a funeral that takes the form of a Quaker Meeting for Worship.

I was privileged to be present at a burial in a garden. I had been lodging in the attic flat of the house of Esma and Joy. Esma was in hospital and we never met. But I knew that he was dying; Joy spent much of her time at the hospital; their two sons spent that time digging their father's grave. The days of preparation imbued the house with not sadness but a profound solemnity; the digging of the grave such a natural devotional act.

On the day I left, they buried Esma in the garden. The ceremony was utterly beautiful; a Quaker Meeting in glorious sunshine, attended by relations and friends. Words were spoken, flowers scattered and at the end we all held hands in a circle round the open grave. He was buried between an old plum tree and a new one, in a plot of land that had already been the burial ground for a badger, a sparrow hawk, several baby birds, an owl and a shrew. The plot of ground is separate from the house, and the family plans to separate it legally so that the land may remain a green space.

I did not know Esma, but I know that he was blessed by the manner of his send-off. The end of his journey from the womb to the earth.

And for some cultures it is death itself that is a homecoming, a return to the land of the ancestors.

The Chinese rootedness in his own native place, and his deep dislike of leaving his ancestral home, were aspects of the importance he attached to family. His devotion to his home village was an extension of his filial piety. To show care for aged parents in life, to mourn them properly in death, to perform rites before the ancestral shrine, to make ceremonial visits to the ancestral grave – these were a man's principal filial duties, virtually impossible to discharge if one lived away from home... Every family that had any means at all would have a graveyard of its own, and if a man should die away from home, no effort would be spared in transporting the corpse back to the ancestral home (Pan, 21).

For Native American tribes, the land and the spirit of ancestors are central. "This was their land, this was the land of their ancestors. Crazy Horse once said, 'Out there,' and he spread his arms in a wide circle, 'out there lie my people. One does not sell where his people lie'" (Chapman, 44).

I have no nostalgia for houses I have lived in. When I pass them, it is with indifference or mild interest that the magnolia is flowering, or that they have mended the back gate. As with the death of a human being, the spirit, the relationships that made it precious, have left the physical entity.

Maeve, on the other hand, yearns for her childhood home. Elderly now, she says,

> I long to go home, to the place in Ireland where we were. I made a noise when I went home. I raced in and played the piano. We had sixteen cats on the farm; all the familiar things, and I raced around even when I was twenty. And my mother, she was great.
>
> And it's all gone. I went back to my home last year. It was a lovely house with big windows, lovely walls, a wicket gate. It's all destroyed, the walls have gone. They've turned the back of it into a bar. I was shattered and my friend who came with me, she wept. My parents left when I was thirty – I didn't want to farm and there was no one else, so they had to leave.

I asked if where she lives now is home. She didn't answer but said, "It has a lovely atmosphere. It was someone's home. I always felt that. They were good people, the people who lived here. I worried that maybe I wouldn't live up to it."

Rabbi Lionel Blue also yearns for a way of life that has gone.

Coming back to London after the Second World War, he found a bomb hole where his house had been, and the local synagogues boarded up. On BBC radio's *Thought for the Day*, he said, "My home died but it remains my home. Since then I have lived in houses."

6

The O of inclusiveness

Community

The Alternatives to Violence Project (AVP) is a conflict resolution programme made up of experiential exercises, a workshop usually run over a weekend or several days. The "building blocks" are affirmation, communication, co-operation and community-building, and conflict resolution. Some time ago, I was one of the facilitators for a workshop in a young offenders' institution. It was one of the most challenging groups I have worked with: "in our faces", literally challenging us and our agreed guidelines throughout the four days we were together. On the first day they were vociferous in their scorn.

"What do you know about what we live with, what we have to put up with?"

"You don't live where we do. It's a rubbish world."

We listened. It was true.

On the fourth day, somewhat drained, I led an exercise called "Image a Better Community". Participants are asked to get into groups of about five, and together consider the kind of community that they would be content to live in. Then, on a large piece of paper, they are asked to draw it.

"Right," I said, "you told us that you live in a rubbish world that none of us would want to live in. What kind of world would you like to live in, would you like your kids to live in? Think about how you would deal with work, food, children, crime, transport and so on. Talk about it, then draw it."

It was a transformative experience for us and, it seemed, for them. With great concentration they drew in their groups worlds with trees and green spaces, with room for education and play, houses with open doors, a river with fish, animals in the field, families, children, fruit to pick and crops in the fields. It was a world of harmony and peace; they were completely lost in these worlds and in the experience of working as a group, and they didn't want to stop. When one young man drew a naked woman, the others in his group hurriedly put clothes on it, out of "respect" for the women facilitators!

Asked to think of one step they could take to move towards creating the community they had drawn, they wrote their pledges on post-it notes, and stuck them on the drawings: "I will give up drugs." "I will be nice to my mum."

Increasingly in Western cultures, people live alone. In Britain, nearly a third of all households are made up of one person, and many are isolated, in flats, houses, little boxes. They may live in streets, villages or towns, but are cut off from their neighbours by walls, fences, and a personal wish or social pressure not to be disturbed or to interfere. Elderly or infirm people may go for days without talking to anyone. Young mothers may have little adult company. "Motherhood", said one woman, "is exile." Those with sufficient money may live in big houses, detached from others. The dream is for bigger and bigger, and surrounded by more and more land – ridding ourselves of troublesome neighbours, the cheek-by-jowl stimulation and conflict of other people. Separation, not relationship.

In Western society, the days of living with extended family are largely past. Susan regretted the loss of community when the family moved from "Dickensian" rented rooms in a square where many members of her family lived to a council flat. When she was a child, even in 1960s London, no one locked their doors, though you didn't go into friends' flats; you waited on the doorstep. In the big house in which she now lives in the same area, she doesn't know her next-door neighbours: some "have problems, alcoholics," some have recently sublet.

Community, where it exists, goes against the trend of isolation and self-sufficiency.

A community is where they know your name and where they miss you when you are not there... society with a human face (Sachs, 54, original italics).

On the basis of this, I live in community – and am rather surprised to hear myself say so. It has not generally been my experience. The first three years of my married life were spent in villages in Wiltshire: the pastoral idyll, but isolated. I was a Londoner, and had left behind job, friends, family and familiar surroundings to stay at home with my new baby while my husband was out at work. Not surprising, then, that I was lonely, but at 23 I had thought I could do anything. I felt more at home in our next house in a medium-sized town – plenty of kindred spirits – but the house itself was on a busy road. Despite living there for six years, we did not know our neighbours. The same was true of our first London house: we knew people in the neighbourhood, but only one of the people in our busy street.

When I came to stay here in a rag trade area in central London – intending it to be a very temporary stay – my neighbours in the basement and on the top floor remembered me from the years I had worked there in what was then my office. It had been six years since I had seen them, but I was warmly welcomed. One now has my keys, and when I was ill my new neighbour downstairs gave me her phone number in case I needed anything. When the news was breaking of the London bombings of July 2005, which all took place within a mile or so of us, I sat upstairs with my neighbour and her baby and in the comfort of each other's presence watched the events unfold on her television. I discuss the cricket with the newsagent, chat to other shopkeepers, to the owners of the local café, to the postman and the road sweeper – yes, it feels like a community. Strange, because it is not a residential area, but there are enough of us to look out for each other. Today, popping out to the local shops, I bumped into a Scottish woman I have known for years, and who calls me "hen". She was a drinker that frequented the Christmas shelter we ran for homeless people in south London, and I come across her from time to time. Last time I saw her she had moved into a hostel, just begun to sell the *Big Issue,* and was worried sick about her partner who she thought was dying. Today, I bought a magazine from her and heard that her partner is fine. We know enough of each other to have a conversation, and to care. We are neighbours.

Big cities like London are not renowned for their friendliness – indeed their anonymity can be part of the attraction – but my experience is shared by many in what can feel like a series of local "villages". Big cities can be a good place to be on long summer nights, when people potter about in their gardens and stroll about in shirt-sleeves. One woman talked of the pleasure of windows thrown open and hearing the snatches of conversation and music: "You know who your neighbours are."

Chris and his wife have lived in the same house in the East End of London, a largely Indian and Bangladeshi neighbourhood, for twenty-one years – the longest Chris has ever lived anywhere. His sense of home includes the neighbourhood. Neighbours on both sides have renovated their houses recently: "We worked things out, on the whole in a friendly manner. Home", he said, "is a place and a series of relationships."

Jo and Richard have lived in the same flat for over forty years. They brought up their children there amid other families: babysitting, caring for each other, was a natural part of life in the building. Jo says, "The reason I feel so rooted here is because so many of the others have been here as long as I have." About five years ago, a vine "arrived" at their third-floor flat balcony, having been planted some years before by the ground-floor resident. "Two years of wonderful grapes", then the residents two floors down, finding their light obscured, cut it back "viciously" and it disappeared. After gentle conversations it's back: a re-established connection between neighbours.

When Gill moved into a new house in south London recently, she was met by a welcoming committee of half a dozen neighbours, all of different nationalities: from Lithuania, Holland, Spain, the Caribbean, Poland. Some have lived there for over 40 years and certainly consider themselves to be at home. An Irish woman in the street celebrated her thirtieth birthday by holding a street party. As far as she knows, Gill is the only one in the street to have been born in London.

Andrew is a hairdresser, working, and previously living, in London. He is forty, married with one small son, and living now on the south coast. When they returned from holiday recently, neighbours welcomed them; it was good to be home. Indeed, Andrew says that since he's lived there he's had no real sense of "home" being the house he lives in. It's the community. And "natural unforced, simple happiness". He has never experienced it before, not even as a child in his family "home".

Relationships with neighbours are not always so harmonious. Thin walls, loud music and differing patterns of work can contribute to stressful living. On some estates, vandalism, graffiti, racism, bullying and fear of crime are rife. Some elderly people are afraid to go out at night. Noise, lack of consideration and aggressive behaviour can turn an otherwise ideal environment into an unhappy experience.

A woman responding to a BBC Radio programme wrote:

I moved to this flat in a former council block three months ago. At most I have had one week of nights without major disruption because of dogs barking, people having parties or visitors all night, doors slammed, couples having noisy sex or fighting. If all people living in poorly insulated flats behave as though they lived in their own castles, i.e. in complete and utter disregard of those living nearby, then I'm not surprised everyone wants to have their own house.

And increasingly we don't know our neighbours. Busy working lives and "minding our own business" mean that in some places we rarely interact with those living near by. In smaller communities, a cheery greeting of passers-by may be more the norm but in many towns in the USA, for instance, where the car culture is ingrained, the passers-by are enclosed in vehicles, and no greetings are exchanged.

Caroline, in Holland, does not know her neighbours. When the children, now teenagers, were growing up, they needed a bigger house and she and her husband could no longer afford to live in Amsterdam. They moved from their family home to Hilversum, to a large comfortable house on a secure estate in wooded surroundings – not quite a gated estate, she says, but maybe with a similar feel. Everyone is preoccupied with their own lives; she is not part of a community – she hasn't even tried. She has not felt at home since they moved there twelve years ago, but it is a practical place in which to bring up children, and reasonably convenient for her daily commute into Amsterdam. In busy lives we make compromises.

A few years ago I spent three months self-catering in a little room in a small South African town where I was one of very few white residents. Local colleagues told me I was not safe, so for the first couple of weeks I was accompanied everywhere. After a while it became obvious that I had been accepted, and my minders relented. One day, a young woman came up alongside me and asked me why I was walking alone.

"Why are you?" I countered.

"I'm going to work," she said, surprised into stating the obvious.

"So am I," I said, and we laughed.

People began to know who I was and what I was doing. I was called *sizi* (sister) on the streets. On my return to the UK I suffered withdrawal symptoms. No one calls me "sister" here!

Paul and I met on a train to Kent, a place he often visits.

Although he now lives in London, home is still the area in which he was brought up and in which his sister lives. "It's a class thing," he says. He can always recognise someone from North Kent: there's a sympathy, an understanding. He feels much more at home with the people who frequent his sister's pub than the people he mixes with in London. Brought up in pubs, he loves the noise, the bustle, the sociability. When he was growing up he had a vision of what an adult man was: Brylcreemed hair, a gold bracelet. The men he sees in the pub are still like that, comfortable and familiar.

Pine Ridge is an Oglala Lakota Native American reservation in South Dakota. At nearly 3,500 square miles, it is one of the largest reservations – and the poorest community – in the US. Nearly half its residents live below the Federal poverty level; the infant mortality rate is five times the national average. Many of the families have no electricity, telephone, running water, or sanitation.

In 2003 I was asked to join three North American women in a visit to Pine Ridge. Kathleen runs an organisation called Mission of Love, dedicated to the support of indigenous peoples all over the world, and is one of the few white people trusted to go on to the reservation. Her organisation and a number of volunteers were to build the first native hospice in North America; they have also supplied housing packs for residents to build, and help others build, their own houses.

The distances on the reservation are enormous – we travelled 2,000 miles in six days – and many of those with diabetes and needing dialysis cannot afford the gas to get to hospital in the nearest town. One of my colleagues, a nurse who has revisited several times and is making a documentary about the reservation, wrote that "the population [is] suffering from diabetes, heart disease, and basically those who are dying having to do so on a dirt floor. It was hard to believe I was in the heart of the USA; even in third-world countries I had not seen that type of poverty. In visiting the people I came to the realization nothing had changed in over a hundred years."

I wrote in my journal,

> What a privilege it is to be accepted into the heart of a people who let so few in, rightly being suspicious of the white people who have treated, and continue to treat, them with such ruthlessness. K is clear that ethnic cleansing is going on – the appalling health care, the thousands of homes with black mould that develops spores inhaled into the lungs of the people. The average age of mortality is 45. Diabetes from the substandard diet doled out by the government, without fresh veg. The black mould develops as a result of houses built with basements and no ventilation.

Nonetheless, Rick Williams, a historian, educator and youth advocate from Pine Ridge, writes,

> If you came onto our reservation you would find people that really care about each other. People who have a spirit that is indefinable in any other context of American society, a spirit whose center is freedom… the reservation is home; it is where physically, spiritually, emotionally and psychologically you're safe – the harmful things that are there differ from those that exist outside the reservation because they're not race-based or hate based. Despite all the things you might hear about reservations, for me it's a wonderful place to be – it's home and there's no place like it. There's no place else in the world I can go to and be embraced by my relatives and where time doesn't make any difference.
>
> …Although there's a tremendous amount of poverty, you won't have trouble finding anything to eat or somewhere to stay on the reservation. People will take care of your basic

needs... somehow they'll find a place for you on the floor, or in the corner because there's always room for one more (Chapman, 126).

Building community

Community can be created through a structured residential approach. Gerry has lived in a housing co-operative in London for nearly thirty years; he was in near the beginning, at the development phase. In those days there were generous grants, so they have been able to keep the rents low. There are 24 units in nine buildings; each tenant also has a share in the ownership, which he gives up when he leaves. It is run on completely mutual lines, and is self-managed without staff. People rarely leave; there is very little turnover, and no one can make a profit out of it. All pay towards a collective thirty-year mortgage. When the co-operative was set up, the council (then the Greater London Authority) based payments on what the original tenants felt they could afford over thirty years. In that way the rent has remained fair.

Cohousing is a way of living which brings individuals and families together in groups to share common aims and activities while also enjoying their own self-contained accommodation and personal space. There are four fully-established cohousing communities in the UK, with an increasing number of groups seeking sites and many individuals seeking a group to join.

Cohousing communities are a means of compensating for the alienating effects of modern life where neighbours don't recognise each other and where day-to-day collaboration is minimal. They offer particular benefits for children in terms of secure play-space and shared activities with their peers. Older people can also find companionship and mutual support in such communities.

The Barracks estate in Salford includes a beautiful square of art deco red-brick dwellings built round a garden. It was built in

1900-1904 as council housing – then seen as a desirable way of life, with early residents being largely professionals such as doctors and teachers.

As part of the much bigger Ordsall estate, it was to become one of the toughest inner-city areas in the country, with a downward spiral of vandalism, muggings, arson and murder. Unlike other parts of the country, the local area suffered from under-demand; empty houses deteriorated, were vandalised and often burnt down. The whole of one side of the old square is now made up of modern replacements. During the period 1988 to 1991 the whole area was emptied and refurbished and, attracted by a subsidy, incomers moved in to the street, Coronation Street, reserved for sale to first-time buyers, some of them owner-occupiers. But the incomers did not relate to the estate and were seen as fair game by some of the people on the estate. Intimidated or the victims of negative equity, few have stayed long. Properties were then bought by buy-to-let landlords, and many let to students and eastern Europeans. The high turnover means that properties are not well looked after and no one cares for their gardens, which have grown wild and become a haven for butterflies.

The refurbishment had been the result of a brave campaign in the mid 1980s by a group of women who decided that they shouldn't have to live like that and who badgered the council until they gave in and agreed to refurbish the estate and reserve half of it for a tenant management co-operative. They were assisted by people from the church and housing professionals. In 1988, when the whole estate was still empty and being refurbished, Jonathan came in as a development worker to help turn it into a going concern. He became so attached that he and his family decided to stay, bought a three-bedroom house in one of the roads not managed by the co-op and, twenty years later, he is still co-ordinator. Over the years Jonathan considers that the co-op has been "quite a powerful influence for good" in the area.

When he showed me round, one example was the much-used play equipment installed in the garden three years ago. Because of the fear of vandalism, it was the first in the whole Ordsall area for eighteen years.

Allocations to co-op housing are made according to housing need and a willingness to participate in the co-operative, which might mean attending co-op meetings, helping to fundraise or serving on one of its subcommittees. Rents in the houses managed by the co-op are the same as for other council housing. Why, then, I asked, would anyone choose to live in the co-op? "Take a look," said Jonathan, "at the streets we manage, and the ones managed by the council." There are stricter rules, he said, for the benefit of living in a place that looks and feels better, and the support given to anyone who has problems.

The estate as a whole is still problematic; the supermarket closed because people walked out without paying; the library closed because of a mugging, then was "arsoned". We passed a boarded-up house where a murder had taken place – the council does not want to re-let it. But, in an otherwise barren area, the Barracks Estate, at least the co-operative's part of it, has become a tiny enclave of participation. Realising that everyone has something to contribute, expecting people to contribute, has a strong impact on people's self-esteem. People respond; it marks the beginnings of community.

The whole area is changing. The council is intending to expand Ordsall estate from 2000 to 8000 properties. There is, as Jonathan says, diversity of tenure; but there is virtually no contact between different groups. There is an entrenched culture of allowing children to be completely unsupervised. They are rude, throw stones at him and others, and can get caught up in more serious violence. Jonathan remembers one evening seeing about fifty children in balaclavas being instructed by a local criminal. They either grow out of it, he says, or end up in the criminal justice system. There is a "lads'" club, but otherwise not much intervention to change destructive attitudes and behaviour. Unlike some other socially deprived areas, there is little resident participation, other than in and around the co-operative itself.

The irony for a man who has done so much to create community in the area is that in the street where Jonathan lives, the turnover is so great that he barely knows his neighbours. It is, he says, the opposite of community.

Feeling at home is not confined to the four walls of your house; community is not restricted to people living close to each other. People find a sense of belonging in groups of like-minded people and may find community in many parts of their life, whether it be the golf club, the local pub or café, a reading group, a religious organisation or a football team. Zoe, in London in her twenties, feels that neighbourhood community has gone. "If I didn't have other networks, I'd be alone."

Work

The vast majority of people work in a different place from where they "live" and, given the amount of time we spend at our workplaces, little thought has been given to how we feel in them. No one I talked to mentioned the office as somewhere they felt to be home, rather somewhere to escape from. Nonetheless, many in our workaholic culture spend more waking hours at work than in any other place; status in Western society is largely defined by the job you do; identity is closely bound up with work. Social life may revolve round work colleagues, forming a community of a kind – not always people we would choose to be with, but then one of the definitions of community is a group of people that one hasn't chosen.

In a culture where "hot-desking" is on the increase, one woman talked of the importance of personalising your space at work. Especially in her work as a social worker, where she and her colleagues go out on a regular basis to deal with stressful situations in different places, it is important to bring a little bit of self to the workplace territory. People find different ways to "self-actualise" in that space. One of her colleagues is surrounded by pink; others may have photos of family on the desk, a bottle of whisky in the drawer.

> Why should the people of our culture choose to use the word "live", which, on the face of it, applies to every moment of our working lives, and apply it only to a special portion of our lives: that part associated with our families and houses. The implication is straightforward. The people of our culture believe that they are less alive when they are working than when they are at home; and we make that distinction subtly clear, by choosing to keep the word "live" for those places in our lives where we are not working.

There is a "widespread cultural awareness of the fact that no one really 'lives' at his place of work" (Alexander, 1977: 223). Are they dead?

Community is not confined to a few like-minded individuals. As the columnist Deborah Orr so graphically reminded us when reporting on the stabbing of a young black boy who lived across the road from her, people can live side by side but in different worlds. The divisions are not necessarily geographical and it is not only those without a roof over their heads or those who come to our shores who are treated with prejudice. Black friends living in the same neighbourhood may not feel as safe as their white neighbours; people with mental or physical disabilities experience the same town, suburb, village, the same country, in a very different way from others living near by.

Poverty and inequality make exclusion endemic in Western societies. Richard Wilkinson, professor of social epidemiology, has done some invaluable work on the effects of inequality on the wellbeing of societies. However rich a country is, it will still be more dysfunctional and violent if the gap between social classes grows too wide. Poorer countries with fairer wealth distribution are healthier and happier than richer, more unequal nations. More unequal societies have lower life expectancy, worse mental health, higher homicide rates, more obesity, and higher teenage birth rates. Children do less well at school, drug problems are more common, a higher proportion of the population is imprisoned, people trust each other less, and community life is weaker.

And in the UK and US the gap between rich and poor is growing. Life expectancy in rich nations correlates precisely with levels of equality. So Greece, with half the GDP per head, has longer life expectancy than the US, the richest and most unequal country with the lowest life expectancy in the developed world. The stress of living at the bottom of the pecking order has a greater impact than poverty itself.

Unless we face the problems in our communities, and attempt to bring troublesome neighbours into them, we will continue to exacerbate troubled and violent behaviour. By handing wrongdoers over to the police and the judiciary, we alienate them further and remove the human faces from those who are then labelled "criminals" or "offenders" and excluded from the community. We are not talking about a tiny, marginal minority of "others". It is estimated that at least twenty percent of the UK working population has a criminal record and one in three men under the age of 30 have criminal convictions. They may live next door. Nearly all people who have been in prison come out and live among us. Most serve sentences of just a few months and then have to adjust to being "on the outside". They are not "offenders": their offences are just part of their human identity. "Crime" is what we decide to criminalise, and in the UK in the past ten years, 3,000 offences have been added to the statute books.

Criminalising actions distances us from those who perform them, absolves them and us from responsibility. And how we decide to deal with crime is a reflection of the values of our society. Restorative justice, in which victim, offender and local community come together to face what has happened, or community courts in which local residents are involved in decisions made, have shown positive results, but are still a tiny part of the criminal justice system.

In general we shut people away in separate institutions, mostly in places inaccessible to their friends and families, and mostly without the resettlement help necessary to transform broken lives. People leave prison without homes, without jobs, with worse family relationships and worse mental health than when they went in. It is not surprising that most of them return, and that significant numbers of people take their own lives in prison, because they have come to believe that those lives are no longer worth living.

The USA imprisons more per head of population than any other country, more even than China or Russia. The UK imprisons more per head of population than any other country in Europe. In 1981, Canadian Quakers recorded their conclusions about prison:

The prison system is both a cause and a result of violence and social injustice. Throughout history the majority of prisoners have been the powerless and oppressed. We are increasingly clear that the imprisonment of human beings, like their enslavement, is inherently immoral, and is as destructive to the cagers as to the caged.

7

Broken circles

Not at home

A house is not always a home. Humans are imperfect beings, and we relate imperfectly. Guilt, it seems, is a natural condition of parenthood – at least in the West. But most people muddle through, and provide a loving environment for children to thrive, a context from which they may explore and eventually leave.

How do children establish a sense of home when they are separated from their families? The boarding school tradition is ingrained in the English way of life: our European neighbours are horrified to hear that some children are sent away as early as six years of age. Some thrive; many do not, and suffer horribly from homesickness. My mother thought it would be good for me to go to a boarding school at thirteen: my brother was a good deal older, and there were difficulties at home. I refused: I did not want to be sent away. My place was with the family at home, whatever the problems.

Homesickness figures largely in boarding school experiences. Fay, who spent the first years of her life in Africa, was sent to boarding school in England at the age of eight. Girls were not allowed to write home for the first eighteen months. The first couple of years were terrible; afterwards she "got used to it". Jo spent two years at a co-educational boarding school that was in crisis. The headmaster was having a breakdown; the atmosphere, she said, was "scary" and she was desperately unhappy. Bullying was rife – the favourite punishment: rubbing girls' faces with boot polish. She still remembers the twice-monthly Sunday nights when they came back from the few hours allowed with parents, and sat in assembly: rows of girls sobbing. Homesickness was a physical pain. A pain around the stomach, a constant ache. "The problem is, you always feel there's something wrong with you." That it's your fault. Fortunately Jo was moved after two years, but it took a long time to adjust. Some girls, she knew, were badly damaged by the experience.

Eudora, on the other hand, made boarding school her home. Sent away at ten, with the discovery that her family was not one she would have chosen, the pupils and teachers at school were home and family to her for the next eight years. She expressed her thoughts at the time as: "I don't really have a family; this school is my family."

It is common in some cultures to give children away, in order to give them a better chance. I met a disabled young woman from Lesotho who had been given to her aunt as a baby. She was one of many children; her aunt had none, and it seemed the natural thing to do; she could not remember if her disabilities had begun before she was given away, or later. And in England I met a teacher who had come to the UK with her aunt in 1981. Her mother went back to Trinidad, giving her to her childless aunt "so that she could have a better life". It was, she said "very hard". As she was not entitled to go to a state school, her aunt had to pay for private schooling out of a nurse's wages.

However happily settled, children who have been adopted often have a deep need to trace their roots, to find their birth mother, to understand why they had been given up for adoption. Was it that they were not wanted?

Our understanding of the importance of familial relationship is relatively recent. Many children living in London during the Second World War were evacuated, sent away from their families to stay with strangers in the country. Some were even sent abroad. Stephen, who was only two at the outbreak of war was sent with his baby sister to Canada, looked after by an aunt. When they returned, some years later, establishing relationships again was not easy; the repercussions of that separation continued well into adult life. At about the same age, my brother was sent from Egypt, where my parents were living during the war, to Palestine, as it was considered a safer place to be.

Sometimes the environment in which children live is very far from a nourishing home. One woman talked of teaching music in a school for the children of rich, often famous people, some of whom went through rapid divorces. Children would be left at school early in the morning, and at night go "home" to a different place. They suffered from a lack of concentration; could not learn. They had no stability from which to thrive. Another teacher said that those who were cared for mainly by au pairs were among the most disturbed children in her school. There was little stability as au pairs came and went, sometimes because of the jealousy of the mother who resented her children's attachment to another woman. For the child, each time it was like losing a mother.

Many children have to cope with unstable, disruptive home conditions, and home is not a place of safety. Some fall by the wayside with a serious impact on their health and education. There is an impact, too, on their own ability to parent. Prisons, providing, as they often do, a net for the failures of the outside community, sometimes offer parenting skills for the young people in their care, many of whom have children. The more I work with men and women in prison, the clearer it becomes that if support had been given when they were children, they would not have ended up behind bars.

Care

Francesca worked for some years as a local co-ordinator for The National Pyramid Trust, selecting under-achieving children in the primary schools of a rural area for an after-school club run by volunteers. The children who caused concern to teachers, nurses or educational psychologists were often the quietest: the sort, as one teacher put it, whom you wouldn't know were there unless you took the register. The volunteers worked with four groups of ten 7-9 year olds, who attended the club for ten weeks, and were given the kind of attention that other children expect to have at home. Francesca found that many of the children came from families in which drugs were a regular feature or the mother was involved in prostitution. In each group of forty there would be at least one whose father or mother was in prison; some came from Traveller families and had not attended school on a regular basis; and some were children of pressurising parents, such as school governors. Although from the same year group, children often didn't know each other, and there were levels of discrimination – "I'm not playing with her; she smells" – that disappeared as the group bonded.

Sometimes, the struggle proves too much, and social workers consider that children can no longer stay in violent or unstable homes; they then have to make the difficult decision to take children away from their families, and put them in the care of the local authority. On 31st March 2007, 60,000 children were in the care of local authorities in England, of whom about 70% were with foster parents, and 30% in a children's home.

In Bulgaria struggling mothers are encouraged to leave their babies in hospital, particularly if the children are disabled, there being little provision for disability in the community. If they are not collected within a year they may be adopted without the parents' permission. Helena, a trainer of social workers, went to Bulgaria for a year's Voluntary Service Overseas, and found a number of huge orphanages, many of them run under the auspices of the Ministry of Health, and very medically oriented. Helena visited one in a vast Soviet block, and in one room found about ten babies of about nine months old, all sitting equidistant from each other, very well dressed and clean – and silent. She said they had little sense of attachment and weren't developing normally. "Still," the staff said, "they're better off than at home;

at least they are fed." In the USA, too, a number of states have "safe-haven" laws allowing the handing over of babies to the government without risk of prosecution. A recent law in Nebraska, however, although intended to protect vulnerable babies, includes all children under 18, with the result that a number of parents are bringing their "unmanageable" older children into government agencies.

The use of the word "care" often in combination with the word "home" can disguise a mode of life that is far from either. In the UK young people from the "care" system are highly represented in the homeless population, and in prison. At the young offenders institution at Feltham, over half have come from "care". The problems may not be entirely of the system's making, but many local authorities do not fulfil their constitutional responsibilities. Children's homes and foster parents struggle to provide the consistency of care that often severely traumatised children need. Some children have had such bruising experience of "family" that they refuse to be placed with foster parents, preferring the anonymity of a care home. Some, never having experienced it, cannot even cope with kindness. Some equate love with violence, which is all they have ever known.

The system in the UK is beset with problems, not least of which are a lack of social workers and a shortage of foster carers, especially those from ethnic minority backgrounds. The arrival of unaccompanied children seeking asylum has added to the pressure. According to a report by Bernados, the number of foster homes that young people had lived in varied from one to thirty, with half having lived in more than four. Such a disruptive way of life means little continuity of schooling, with resultant poor attainment. Nearly half of those surveyed said that no one went to parents' evenings, sports days or other events.

Rosemary was a full-time foster carer for about thirteen years. During that time she and her husband, Robert, fostered 43 children, occasionally for a twenty-four-hour emergency, sometimes for several years, usually for a few months. They had a big house, and so were able to take sibling groups. On one occasion they were fostering six children at once, two of whom went home at weekends. They have two children of their own.

Rosemary remembers as a child dreaming of looking after children, so when she met Robert, a social worker who wanted to foster, the decision was made. They took their training seriously both before and throughout the time they were fostering and both trained in family therapy. They worked hard in each case to move the children back "home" to their birth parents, and on most occasions succeeded, though she remembers sad occasions when that was not the case.

One boy – let's call him Leo – came to them when he was about ten. He had been arrested for stealing, and he was a smoker. Robert used to roll up cigarettes with Leo, and used it as an occasion to chat, suggesting, for instance that he might be able to save up for a much-wanted game if he didn't smoke. They were making headway. But Leo wanted to see his mother, and the social worker forbade a visit until the mother had had a meeting with her. So every now and then Leo ran off to spend a few days with his mother, unsupervised. Despite Rosemary's suggestion that she could take him for a supervised visit to his mother, the social worker refused. The upshot was that Leo re-offended, and was sent to a secure accommodation. When Rosemary visited him, she found he was being given cigarettes for good behaviour.

The children in their care were part of the family. When two Muslim children came who were not allowed to watch television, the whole family ate Halal meat, and no one in the family watched television. They talked instead. Over the years, Rosemary said, there were many good times, and some very challenging ones. One three-month old baby was coming off drug dependency and woke every hour; one girl came to Rosemary's bedroom every night to wake her up. Eventually they learnt that she had been told that she had been moved because her alcoholic birth mother wouldn't wake up.

Rosemary gave lessons to excluded children; she liaised with birth parents about what their children needed and, when the children left, she made a "loving and caring cake". There was a candle for everyone who cared about the child – a teacher, her mother, friends at school. It was an affirming ending to their relationship, a closing. Foster carers are not encouraged to stay in touch with the children, and Rosemary has hardly ever heard how the children she has cared for have got on.

They have been asked to adopt, but were clear that they didn't want to do that; they were happy with their own two children. In the end, the fostering all became too much. There was never a break. "If you are successful," says Rosemary, "you are used all the time. Sometimes there are calls at two in the morning." Looking back, she considers that some decisions made about the children in their care were not sensible. The system did not listen to the people who knew the children well. She also considers that the needs of the birth children of foster carers should be taken more into account. They tried to foster only children who were younger than their own but, even so, difficulties arose, especially when some of the foster children ganged up on one of her sons, and the social worker refused to intervene.

"It was our life and for the most part we did love it. But it wasn't without problems, and mostly it was the Social Services."

Many foster homes are homes indeed: providing a loving and inclusive environment for children who often present very challenging behaviour. Others treat those they foster differently. Some will not take their foster children on family holidays. One child said, "The others get the full Monty for breakfast; I just get Rice Krispies."

The care that Robert and Rosemary took to involve birth parents in decisions about their children is unusual. In 2008, a report examining birth parents' views found that most feel their children were looked after well by the council but feel left out of their offspring's lives. The report highlighted "the sense of despair, guilt, anger and failure that many parents feel". Some of the parents described having a child in care as being "a living nightmare, hell on earth" and "a never-ending battle".

"Reunification" (the return of children to their birth parents) is often badly managed. Little work is done either with the child or with the parents to prepare them for what can be a highly emotional event. If no support has been given to deal with the original problems, the likelihood is that the same problems will recur, setting up the same sense of failure among the parents and increased insecurity in the children. And sometimes foster parents are given no warning that the child is to leave them. One foster mother, who had been fostering a child for a long time, told of her experience of sending her foster daughter to school one day. When she did not return at the usual time, she contacted the school to be told, "Oh, she's gone home". There was no preparation, no chance to say goodbye.

A family support worker told me that when children are taken away, a plan for permanence is developed with the birth parents: this might either be for rehabilitation, or for adoption. She felt that the system was geared against birth parents, many of whom were women on their own, some with learning difficulties. It is a time of great distress, and the system does not lend itself to compassion.

Before the Children's Act 2000, local authorities had a legal responsibility for children only until the age of eighteen. They now have a duty of care for those young people continuing in education until the age of 24. Given that 40% leave care with no qualifications, those who continue into further or higher education are rare. One girl, who had lived with foster parents for many years, went to university, and had nowhere to go in the holidays, nowhere to leave her possessions. Her foster parents had taken in other children, and there was no room for her.

Occasionally foster children stay on. An extreme case is the woman who is still with her foster carer family 34 years later at the age of forty; the foster carer is in her eighties and has children of her own. She had always asked for children who wanted a home!

A spate of stabbings in the UK in 2007 and 2008 brought the prevalence of gang culture to the public attention. For young people who are alienated from family and school, gangs offer a form of identity and belonging. United in their association with a territory – a place, even a zip code – they fight to protect their right to it. The Chief Constable of South Wales expressed a view that for some disaffected young people "tribal loyalty has replaced family loyalty and gang culture based on violence and drugs is a way of life".

A Place Called Home (APCH) is a centre for young people based in Los Angeles, founded in 1993. It was created to give young people in danger of gang involvement in the inner city a place where they could come after school, get a snack, do their homework, watch TV, play with their friends, and be with people that care about them – "basic rights that all kids should have". Its mission is to provide at-risk young people with a secure, positive family environment where they can regain hope and belief, earn trust and self-respect and learn skills to lead to a productive lifestyle free of the gangs, drugs and poverty that surround them.

From this fundamental concept, APCH now offers an all-day school, computer lab, music, art, dance, tutoring and mentoring. APCH began working with twelve inner-city children in a basement of a church. It now works out of a 10,000 square foot facility, and has been recognised as a place of neighbourhood excellence.

Refuge

We once lived next door to a rooming house. The woman who

had the room next to our bedroom worked as a barmaid, and came back, usually, in the early hours of the morning. She lived for a while with a man whom I never saw, but with whom she had a combative relationship. I was often woken by their rows – she had a powerful voice – shouting sometimes followed by the sound of a blow and always tailing off into the sound of her crying. Once I met her in the street with her arm in plaster. She was in tears. As I commiserated with her, I learnt that she was crying not because of her injury, but because he had left.

It is not only children who have to leave home. Severe, repeated and systematic violence occurs in at least five of every hundred marriages in Britain. 100,000 women per year seek treatment in London for violent injuries received in the home. In the States, research has found that half of all women will experience some form of violence from their partners during marriage, and that more than one-third are battered repeatedly every year. Even in a violent relationship, it seems surprisingly hard to leave, particularly if a woman has children, and it means taking them away from school and friends, as well as losing the family home.

Stella came to the UK two years ago from Nigeria under a settlement visa "through the man I loved". Her husband – she never named him – brought her and their baby son over after many years of visiting her in Nigeria for a couple of weeks at a time. Their daughter, now twenty, was already studying in Britain. Stella was happy: she loved travel, new people, and was with the man she loved. Within six months of their arrival, she said, her husband changed. In their culture, she explained, a woman has no rights, and has to do what her husband says. Before coming to the UK it had never been a problem, as she had her own life. Once under one roof in England, her husband shouted at her, threatened her, criticised her continually, told her she didn't know how to dress, how to cook, even how to talk. "Whatever I want you to do, you must just do it. You have no right to question me." She knew no one, did not, as she said, "know my left from my right. It was like someone killing you silently." He stopped her going to church, packed up her things, as he did not wish to see them. They did not even share a bed. When he wanted her, he just told her to take off her clothes and threw her on to the bed.

Stella tried to make it work. Her home and her children, she said, were her first priority. Initially he did not want her to work, but she was desperate to get out of the house and eventually found her way to the job centre, and got work as a carer, working at night. Matters came to a head when her husband opened a letter to her daughter from the bank. When her daughter complained, he shouted, "How dare you criticise me," and attacked her. The daughter ran to a friend's house and called the police. He was arrested, but Stella refused to press charges – she said she would sort it out. She found her daughter, brought her back to the house, and together they went on their knees to Stella's husband, and begged his forgiveness. He refused, and became more violent than ever, accusing Stella of disloyalty and threatening her life. He tried to throw her and the children out of the house, and told her she would not get indefinite leave to remain in the country unless she paid him a large sum of money. He told her he would call the police and have her sent back to Nigeria. In the end, she felt that she had no choice, and called the police herself, expecting to be thrown out of the house. When the police arrived, they told her husband to pack his bags, took his house key and gave it to Stella. He was given six months to prove his good behaviour.

Stella was astonished. She had had no idea of her rights, of how things were in Britain. Despite continuing harassment from her husband, eventually the police referred her to the Bede House Association, a charity helping women suffering from domestic abuse and, with their help, she now has the right to remain in the country. She is moving into temporary accommodation, applying for her own home, and hopes to go to college next year. "Thank God, and Bede – if it weren't for Bede I could still be there.

"Home? Home means love and acceptance. Unity. A person [in a family] cannot make home on their own: it takes two. It needs understanding and to be peaceful." The place in which she was living had not been a home. The change in her life "was like going from a slavery camp to freedom". Stella is content too in the UK.

This country is better than Nigeria because women are empowered, and children come first. It's better here because of the encouragement of women, working, making yourself independent. I've never been treated badly in this country. I'm happy with my children. Panic has left me. Now I can smile again.

A refuge is the last resort for women who can't afford to move into alternative accommodation, women who often have become isolated from family and friends by an abusive partner, and whose self-esteem is so low that it is hard for them to pick themselves up. 30,000 women and children stay in refuges in the UK every year.

I visited a short-term emergency refuge in south London, an anonymous wide-fronted modern building in an unremarkable suburban street. I sat with five women in the sitting room, with children playing in the room next door, separated by a glass partition, and listened to their life-stories, to why they are not in homes of their own. All are local, referred by local agencies or by themselves, and allowed to stay for a maximum of four months. None would have chosen to be in the refuge: they find it claustro- phobic, and it reminds them of why they are there. Several said they needed to get out every day, "to see the blue sky and the autumn leaves". All the women I talked to have children, though the eight-bedded building allows for two single women.

Their stories were very different in some respects; in some, shockingly the same: having to ask permission for the simplest things; in one case not being allowed to lock the door of the lavatory.

Mary had been in a violent relationship for five years, being beaten "every week or two". When her jaw was broken, her doctor broke confidentiality and talked to Mary's partner, who locked her in the flat with no clothes for three days. She has finally found another doctor, but is scared now to move away in case she cannot again find someone to trust – something that does not now come easily. When Mary came into the refuge, she was pregnant, but miscarried as a result of the beatings. She had two children: her daughter is with Mary's mother in Ireland, for safety. Her son hanged himself.

She herself had planned to murder her partner, keeping a knife under the mattress. She had not wanted to come to the refuge but "thank goodness", she said, for her key worker. "I'd have been dead or in prison. It was him or me. I was becoming like him." Now she says she's a changed woman.

All I need is my own little place. A bedsit. Somewhere I can shut the door and feel safe. I never got a night's sleep for years. I have a lifeline now. It's not just us that suffers, it's our families. My mother lay awake, thinking I was dead. He was planning to cut me up and feed me to the pigs.

Rachel had been with her partner from the age of 16. Two years ago she moved out and found her own place. But he stalked her, found her, watched the house, put letters through the door, threatening to kill her. She now feels she is away from where he can get her. She wants to be safe.

Valeria and her two children are homesick. She has been in the same relationship for 21 years, and it is her second time in a refuge. Her daughter blames her, misses her friends, her school, her pets. She loves her dad, "and in some ways he is not a bad man," says Valeria, with tears in her eyes. It is hard to give up on family life. She just kept hoping it would get better. "The violence was always a shock to me, and to him." He had made promises after the last time to go to counselling and anger management, but the abuse had gone on, even if it wasn't always physical. He took away the phone, the TV and the post. Valeria, who spoke no English when she came to this country from Russia in 1995, became very isolated. "I have always felt trapped. I don't feel angry, but I don't want the children to grow up thinking this is normal."

"The role of a wife and mother," said Marta, "is to keep the family together." When she came to England from Italy she was young and single. "I travelled, went to Australia, had fun. I then felt I was settling down." After the first year's "honeymoon period", she realised that her husband's drinking was serious. Her parents' health, then her own pregnancy, distracted her from what was going on as first he abused her verbally, then hit her. He promised to seek help, but has not done so. "My father was an alcoholic – it makes you wonder which is the real person. Maybe it is the drunk. I'm hoping my son and his father will have quality time together: it's my son's right."

Marta had a termination in July. She cried as she told me that she felt she had no alternative. She is 32 and wanted more children. "Killing", she said, "was not on my agenda."

For Marta, everything is new, not just the refuge. "I'm here because I have nowhere else to go." She can't afford a privately rented place, so will have to go on benefits, something she never expected to do. "A home is everything. A place where you can feel comfortable, fearless, hear the music, cook the food. If there is too much argument, there is no harmony. There is no home."

Valeria seemed to speak for all of them when she said, "I'm not afraid of anything. I'm not afraid of poverty. I want to live here and now. Problems have made me stronger." Marta added, "It is easy just to blame. You have to forgive them. Then you can heal."

The address of the refuge is, for obvious reasons, secret. If a partner or anyone else turns up and asks for one of the women, security has been breached and the woman is found somewhere else to stay. The refuge does not pretend to be home; it is a temporary respite for desperate women; affords them a breathing space with help from trained staff, and the chance to get housed and start a new life. For all the women I spoke to, home is somewhere, however small, where you can shut the door and be safe.

After many years as professor at Harvard, Yale and Notre Dame in the States, years of talking about God on platforms, Henri Nouwen said he felt uneasy in his heart, and distant from his vocation. He prayed for clarity, and was beckoned into a new life by first a messenger from, then a meeting with, Jean Vanier, the founder of L'Arche, a community for people with learning difficulties and others who share their life. Henri Nouwen records that meeting:

> We met silently at a retreat in which no words were spoken. At the very end Jean said, "Henri, maybe we, our community of handicapped people, can offer a home to you, can offer a place to you where you are really safe, where you can meet God in a whole new way." It was an incredible experience because he didn't ask me to be useful; he didn't ask me to work for handicapped people; he didn't say he needed another priest; he didn't say any of these things. He said, "Maybe we can offer a home to you."

The first thing they asked him to do was to work with a twenty-four-year-old man called Adam, who was very, very handicapped. He couldn't speak. He couldn't walk. He couldn't dress or undress himself. His back was distorted and he suffered from continuous epileptic seizures. And

something happened. I was frightened for about a week, a little less frightened after two weeks. After three or four weeks, I started to realize that I was thinking about Adam a lot and that I was looking forward to being with him. Suddenly I knew something was happening between us that was very intimate, very beautiful and that was of God... Somehow I started to realize that this poor, broken man was the place where God was speaking to me in a whole new way.

Adam taught me a lot about God's love in a very concrete way. First of all, he taught me that being is more important than doing, that God wants me to be with God and not to do all sorts of things to prove that I'm valuable... Here I was with Adam and Adam said, "I don't care what you do as long as you will be with me."

...Then he taught me something else. He taught me that the heart is more important than the mind... I suddenly realized that what makes a human being human is the heart with which he can give and receive love. Adam was giving me an enormous amount of God Is love and I was giving Adam of my love. There was an intimacy that went far beyond words or far beyond activity. I suddenly realized that... God wanted to dwell in his broken person so that He could speak from that vulnerability into the world of strength, and call people to become vulnerable.

Finally, Adam was telling me... that... doing things together is more important than doing things alone. I came from a world that is very much concerned with doing things on your own, but here was Adam, so weak and vulnerable. I couldn't help Adam alone. We needed all sorts of people. We had a person from Brazil, people from the United States,

Canada, Holland – young, old living together in one house around Adam and other handicapped people. Suddenly I realized that Adam, the weakest among us, created community. He brought us together and his needs, his vulnerability, made us into a true community... His weakness became our strength. His weakness made us into a loving community (from a talk "Journey to L'Arche", first broadcast on 1 October 1989).

8

The oneness of O

Borders and belonging

"I am a Jewish writer in the sense of writing forever about the ache to have a home, and then having one, aching to go away thinking that this is not the real one." That's the condition on which we hold our humanity. We all belong to two places. Three even. Here, there, and wherever we're going – heaven, hell, or just oblivion. We English make too much of a meal of the vexations of belonging, terrified of asking immigrants to love it here when they understandably love somewhere else, forgetful of how easy it is to love both... The heart has its allegiances to places as well as to people, and a country is a place and a people.

Howard Jacobson quoting Amos Oz

If few people have much choice about the house they live in, in the West few believe that we have a choice about where we are born, and to whom. A child born in a Rio slum will have a very different life from one born in a brownstone in New York. Health, life expectancy and life chances can vary hugely even within the same town.

Borders

There are some natural geographical borders: a range of mountains, a wide river, oceans, that divide one part of land from another. But humankind, from fear and from possessiveness, creates borders to keep other people out. Gated estates, writ large.

We control entry to our countries with criteria, regulations and checkpoints; some are crossed only with bribery; some are manned by armed guards; others you can walk through with a minimum of fuss. How easy it is also depends on who it is that wants to come in. How smug we feel, walking through the border control of our own country – with barely a backward glance at the long queue of those in the channel marked "other": a queue that might take hours to process, with aggressive questioning, assuming some unnamed guilt, often with an unvoiced racist edge. Having stood in the "other" channel to enter, for instance, Israel and the USA, I know how humiliating it can be. How much more so if you are ordered to strip.

Many of the problems arising in twenty-first-century Africa are the result of artificially created boundaries in its colonial past. Ryszard Kapuscinski describes how, under Bismarck's leadership, European colonialists divided Africa among themselves, cramming "the approximately ten thousand kingdoms, federations and stateless but independent tribal associations that existed in this continent in the middle of the nineteenth century within the borders of barely forty colonies" (47).

And borders change. In my lifetime, the creation of the European Union means that members do not have to show a passport to go from one country to another and, as the EU expands, so the borders within it diminish. The Berlin Wall, which divided one part of Germany from another for twenty-eight years, and was the central symbol of the Cold War between the two super-powers and their allies, came down in 1989 to great scenes of joy and celebration. Germans who would have been shot for trying to cross it just months before were able to move freely in what was once again the same country. In India, sixty years after partition, the border with Pakistan is still disputed, with many families divided, living either side of the Kashmiri Line of Control.

In some parts of the world, borders are continuously shifting, often as a result of arbitrary post-war settlements by other countries, or ethnic conflict. The borders of the country known as Yugoslavia, for instance, changed twice between 1941 and 2006, when it collapsed as an entity, broken up along ethnic lines into a number of separate states. As I write, Russia is talking of "redrawing the map" in its conflict with Georgia over South Ossetia, saying that it is unlikely that South Ossetia will re-integrate with the rest of Georgia. Not surprisingly, this area of the Caucasus is a strategic area and one rich with oil.

Some towns are claimed by one country then another. Garibaldi, the instigator of Italian reunification, was actually born in France. Nice, having belonged for most of its existence to part of what is now Italy, was ceded to the French about ten years before his birth, though it was given back a few years afterwards. In 1860, some years before Garibaldi declared Italian unification, it was given again to the French. Strasburg has been both in Germany and in France; towns now in Slovakia have belonged within living memory to Hungary, then Czechoslovakia. It is not surprising if residents of such towns have a somewhat schizo-phrenic view of their nationality.

Nationality

On the whole we take our national identity for granted. Only when under threat from another country, at times of war, in a sporting contest, or when we ourselves wish to leave our shores for another does it arise. We don't often think what it means to be British or American or Australian.

Despite the globalisation of the market-place, national characteristics still distinguish us. Determined largely by climate, geographical features, our cultural, social and military history, and – where it tallies – ethnicity, the result is a rich diversity of physical and cultural characteristics. Such a wealth of difference is a cause for celebration, but an ingrained fear of the "other" often leads to prejudice, racism and stereotyping jokes. Most peoples identify another group as the butt of racist jokes: the Irish for the English; the Poles for Russians.

Patriotism, however, is no longer fashionable in the West. Flag-waving is suspect in liberal circles because of the implied exclusion of those who do not belong – and certainly in the States notices outside houses proclaiming "Proud to be American" raise the question of how that impinges on those who are from elsewhere. Pride in a country is more prevalent among immigrants, perhaps, because they have a deeper need to establish an identity and know better the value of what they've found than those who take its advantages for granted. Nationality can rarely express the complexities of human identity and belonging.

I have never felt particularly English: in fact for many years I felt foreign, and assumed (wrongly) that I would marry someone from abroad. Nationality, in fact, has not been a large part of my identity. It might have to do with having family from and in different countries. A generation later, Eudora feels much the same. Half German, half English, she was taken to and fro as a child, is trilingual and never felt she belonged in either place.

I've never had a home, a country to call home. I've always felt a foreigner. The problem here is everyone thinks I'm English, and that I should behave like that whereas when I'm in France they think if I'm a bit weird it's because I'm English. I've lived abroad. It doesn't matter where I live.

Another friend said, "I don't feel a strong identity in a country. I prefer to find it in individuals."

Susan is English, but does not think about her national identity, and as she was growing up she thought that such ideas were fading away. Its resurgence has surprised and disturbed her. She considers that the creation of the nation state in the nineteenth century was a disaster, and the recent rise of nationalism regressive, particularly its introduction to areas such as Eastern Europe where people represent a strong mixture of ethnicities. In former Yugoslavia, where she spent a year as a volunteer, she says that strong notions of national identity were deliberately manipulated as a replacement for socialism.

Anna, writing from South Africa, says,

Classification of nationalities and the rigour of the criteria change according to countries we are in. It links to policies on migration, history and colonialism. Identities, categories, shift according to different interests. It is a worrying debate, which recalls the Apartheid era and Nazi Germany. Classification was everything.

Some peoples feel locked into an artificial nationality. Where culture, language and identity are not represented by a nominal nationality, alienation is a natural state, and minorities often feel oppressed. The Kurds, a people who live in Iran, Iraq, Turkey, and Syria as well as in exile in the UK and US, have long wanted their own homeland, as have the Basques, living in the Pyrenean region of France and Spain.

To observe the Basques is to ask the question: What is a nation? The entire history of the world, especially of Europe, has been one of redefining the nation. From pre-Indo-European tribes – all of whom have disappeared, except the Basques, Europe shifted to kingdoms, empires, republics, nation-states (Kurlansky, 5).

The idea of a passport has existed since people began to travel from one country to another. In the United Kingdom, the "Safe Conduct" was at first little more than a note signed by the king or queen asking that the person who held it be allowed to travel freely. Safe Conducts were issued to people of all nationalities and were mentioned as early as an Act of Parliament in 1414.

Since 1858 UK passports have been restricted to United Kingdom nationals, and their importance globally as evidence of nationality has grown as borders tighten to restrict the numbers of people entering the country. Like an address, passports have been taken over by legalism and bureaucracy to prove identity, but they are precious also because of the freedom they bestow· a pass to cross borders, to leave a homeland and – most importantly – to return.

Countries where education is largely influenced by another country can suffer a disjunction between expectations and their lived reality. An Australian friend told me that when she was growing up in Australia in the 1960s, there was a constant hankering after the Northern hemisphere. All the books at school, everything that stimulated the imagination, were European, mostly English. The seasons in Australia seemed "all wrong" because reality was represented by information they got from English books. Christmas "should" be cold.

Philippa says that she has always distrusted patriotism; she finds it suspiciously jingoistic. It was only when she lived abroad for a couple of years that she realised being English was important to her. "It's not about flags and so on; it's about Marmite and Cadbury's and real ale." But while abroad she also felt liberated from the need to support her national team – she doesn't see why sport has to be tied to nationality. But, given the number of people who now opt to have their ashes scattered on football pitches, "their team" is increasingly where people feel their allegiance, that belonging. Tribalism is a force to be reckoned with.

A British cabinet minister famously talked of the "cricket test": asking which team you would support in a match between your country of origin and your adopted country. The implication was that the "wrong" answer meant that you did not belong. Guy would have failed. A young Englishman living in France, he gives "Nice" as his home, but during the 2008

Olympics rooted unashamedly for Britain. "We've made our home in Nice," said his partner, "but we're English." And in a series of interviews with Turkish workers in Germany before a Turkey/German football match, the answers invariably were "Turkey, that's where I come from"; "Turkey, I was born there." One second-generation Turkish German said that he had dual allegiance. Like Howard Jacobson, he recognised that belonging is not so simple.

Complexity, however, is not taken into account by bureaucratic procedure. Now in her eighties, Johanna was born in Poland, picked up by the Germans during the war, and taken to work first in Germany, then in Italy. Hearing Polish spoken, she caught up with the Polish army and after the war was demobbed in the UK. She has never taken British nationality and has no Polish papers, but has been living in the UK for 62 years and has permanent right to remain. Recently, wishing to travel abroad, she applied for travel documents, only to be told that she could not have any papers, nor the right to remain, until Poland had belonged to the EU for five years. She would have to apply to "her country" for a passport.

Rooted

Cheddar Man is the name given to the remains of a human male found in a cave in Cheddar Gorge, Somerset, England, dating from approximately 7150 BC. In the late 1990s, a researcher from Oxford University compared mitochondrial DNA taken from twenty living residents of the village to that extracted from Cheddar Man's molar tooth. It produced two exact matches and one match with a single mutation, thus establishing a genetic link between inhabitants of the village some 9,000 years apart, and an indicator of the stability of the local population.

Even in this era of travel, movement, restlessness and migration, 97% of the world's population live and die in the country in which they were born. Less than half of American people own a passport. Some people are rooted, relate strongly to a particular vicinity or community, have a strong sense of place. For some this is a condition established in childhood: a family inheriting a farm, living in the same house for several generations, people who never leave the village in which they were born. Even today, young people on a south London estate have never been further north than the centre of the city. In many countries that will be the norm. For communities where there is no transport, where people have to walk several miles to fetch water or buy food, travelling beyond the local vicinity is simply not an option. Even where there is choice, people often stay put. My father's family stayed in the same area of London for several generations. Bob and his sister live in the London house in which they were born. When they inherited it, they split it and brought their families up in the two halves.

For others stability is acquired later in life, maybe as a compensation. Cliff's father was a Methodist minister and they moved house seven times before Cliff was 18. He has now lived in the same house for 38 years and has a strong sense of place. He is a local councillor; supports the local football team; always buys local produce. He has become rooted in a place.

A chronicler of the Chinese diaspora writes:

For commitment to one's native place, one's ancestral home, few people could beat the Chinese. The word *hsiang*, which can mean a village, the countryside, one's home town or native place, is one of the most evocative words in the Chinese language, far more emotive than its equivalents in English (Pan, 21).

But rooted communities can be hard to penetrate. In the 1970s, my husband and I arrived as new parents in a Wiltshire village. We simply did not fit in. My husband found companionship in the local pub; I, at home with a baby, found people friendly enough, but it stopped at the front door. As newcomers, we were never accepted, and I was terribly lonely. A friend told me that it took her aunt, moving from one Gloucestershire village to another, ten years to be fully accepted.

Homogenous societies may feel more comfortable, more familiar – we know each other's rules – but finally perhaps they are less exciting, a bit bland. My husband and I decided that we didn't want to stay in those rural surroundings; we didn't want to bring our children up in what was then such a white mono-culture. We wanted to be citizens of the world, not of one small corner of England.

Britain and New World countries are wonderful melting pots of nationalities and languages. There are few people here who can trace several generations of their family back within one country on both sides of the family. We are a mongrel lot and, to my mind, all the stronger for it.

My mother's family is a particularly vivid example of twentieth-century history. Fleeing Russia in the aftermath of the Revolution, she, her mother and brother stayed first with grandparents in Latvia, then moved on to Switzerland. At 21, my mother married a Swiss lecturer, and moved with him to Egypt, where he died. After the war she moved to England with her second husband, my father. Her brother stayed in Switzerland and married first a Frenchwoman, then an Iranian; her cousin, Alec, settled with his mother in France. He married first the daughter of a Frenchman who sheltered him in the war; then a Greek model, then, being sent by the UN to Central America after the war, a Guatemalan woman, and eventually moved out to Guatemala. My brother was born in Egypt; I in England.

A generation later, my nephew has married first a Malay woman, and now a Colombian.

Movement
In societies where there is an abundance of choice, there are

many who feel that neither the stimulus of city nor the peace of country alone seems to be enough. Those with enough money have a foot in each world; are able to embrace both aspects of their desire. It does, however, mean two properties to look after, two sets of essential equipment. So often, I hear, the book or tool or paper that is needed is in "the other place". A couple with places in London and Cornwall think of each as home when they are going there; others, more restless perhaps, might think always that home is in the other place.

Tobias Jones writes about the downside of mobility:

I drive thousands of miles every year to see friends and relatives who live the other side of the country or on the continent. None of us live in the same neighbourhood any more and mobility is the neurotic result. We're never at home for the weekend. I seem to be suffering from an inability to stop and belong. Where I stand used to be the centre of my world, but it's no longer like that. The world has shrunk exponentially and now, instead of feeling at home where I actually am, I imagine home is wherever I'm not (9).

Many ways of life demand movement: long-distance lorry drivers, fishermen, soldiers and diplomats travel as a way of life, often resulting in family separation. A long-haul pilot and his wife found the continual adjustments on his return trips difficult to navigate. For her it was on each occasion a shift from being sole manager and decision-maker to sharing decisions: he in turn needed to ease back into home life.

The ease of travel, and global communication, mean that more people than ever live a peripatetic life. I have met couples each of whom works in a different country, and on Friday nights European train stations and airports are full of men and women returning "home" after a week's work elsewhere. Sean is a taxi driver in London. He lives by the sea in County Clare, Ireland,

and flies back and forth each week. It's an easy journey but when he sets off at 4 am on a Monday morning he says he'd often just like to turn the car round and go home. It won't be for ever. He and his wife are building a house and when it's done, they plan to start a dog kennelling business. They have three dogs of their own and find kennel places hard to find. Kennels are full, he says, of dogs left by the owners while they winter abroad. Another taxi driver, unusually, was a white-haired woman. She and her husband – also a taxi driver – have a little place in Essex, but actually live in Spain. They stay in Spain until the money runs out, then come over and drive taxis till they have enough to go back.

People who spend much of their lives abroad respond in various ways. Some, like Simon, whose work led him to live in many countries, is hugely relieved to have settled in a beautiful sixteenth-century manor house in Kent, and has no wish to go anywhere else. Two sisters who travelled a lot as children had quite different reactions in adult life. One never wanted to move again; the other became an air hostess. A teacher brought to the UK from Trinidad when she was a child was given the chance to go back to Trinidad to live when she was sixteen. She visited, but didn't want to stay. For her, England is home.

In 2002, my then partner and I came back from a year's backpacking round the world. I wrote:

I had been dreading it, filling my emails with fears of a year's paperwork, the descent of responsibility. And typically, as I took the tube from Heathrow home, we were stuck for an hour and a half by a train breaking down in front of us...

But we were greeted by the most beautiful English spring, the loveliness of which I had forgotten: the greenness, the freshness of the trees, and the birdsong. I felt as if I were seeing England anew. Even London, which I had been so keen to leave, so sure that we would move from it on our return, was a pleasure. The multi-cultural richness that we had spoken of abroad, always with some secret negativity about the noise, dirt and overcrowded transport, seemed to be a real wealth, with a texture and variety that was wholly appealing. My flat, which I had always felt had its limitations and was a temporary measure, felt indeed like home. The blackbirds are still here in my little garden, and have been joined by a pair of robins and a pair of wrens; shopkeepers ask if I had a good time. Familiarity is very attractive. How easy it is! (Kavanagh, 2004: 195).

Will Self too enjoys London's diversity:

While I may trot the globe, I still return to a strange kind of urban homeland: a quarter of a mighty world city in which six generations of the male line of my family have now resided. I don't begrudge anyone coming into this Self homeland – on the contrary, the burgeoning of London's immigrant population during my adult life has been a source of delight to me... Black, brown, white – they look like Londoners, they all sound like Londoners. They're perfectly at home here. And so am I (Smolan and Erwitt quoted in the *Independent*, 7 June 2008).

Kim has just moved back to the UK after ten years living abroad. She is in her sixties.

People ask me which country I prefer. It isn't about preferring Britain, it is that it is home. I feel at home in S. Africa, but it's not my home home. A very small example. Some police in South Africa wear one colour uniform, another another. I don't know why. I don't know those kinds of small details. My kids are here, a lot more close friends. It feels right. I am surprised by how important a "home" is to me, having things around me. I'm looking for somewhere to settle, planning for when I'm 85. I have to have a home. I thought I'd be happy going off with a pack on my back.

Many live in one place and hanker after another. Home is often what you think about when you are away from it, and when you get back to it, it isn't what you thought it was.

This was particularly true for Pamela who was born in Australia, then for twenty-five years travelled with her diplomat husband to many developing countries mostly in Africa and the Caribbean. When they finally came back to England, it wasn't what they remembered. Apart from anything else, everyone seemed so white! Only when she went to ethnically mixed areas, into a supermarket full of Indian and Afro-Caribbean people, did she sigh with pleasure and feel at home. But they have settled here for the time being, even if the sun might call them elsewhere in the future.

Pamela said that "home" is not a word she ever uses. Moving every four years, she said that she had given her heart to many places but didn't dare to think of anywhere as "home": such a commitment felt unsafe.

Some never return to the land of their birth: they simply feel they no longer belong.

Migration

Much individual and mass migration, both within countries and internationally, has been in search of work. In the nineteenth century, the Industrial Revolution led to a mass movement from the countryside to the cities. In China what is being called the second industrial revolution is taking place in the twenty-first century at an unprecedented speed. It has been predicted that in the next 25 years, 345 million Chinese will move from rural areas to cities: the biggest migration the world has seen. World-wide, a movement from countryside to cities is a general tendency; many countries cannot keep up with the migration, and many moving to the cities find themselves in penury: living in a slum or on the streets.

Seasonal migration is also common, as people head for towns at times of hardship and return to their villages for the harvest. And families are separated. One member, usually the man, will go to live in another part of the country, returning at weekends, or less frequently. Where a lot of money is to be made, individuals or families are often on the move for years. The recent re-opening of the coal mines in Queensland, Australia, has brought large numbers of people to the area to seek their fortunes. People live in very basic temporary accommodation, moving on to where the pickings are greater. As with the gold rush before it, financially it can be worth it – many earn well over double the national average wage. Emotionally, continual separation and life on the move can take their toll.

Like many other creatures, human beings have always travelled to and lived in countries other than their own. Two million years ago *homo erectus* began its first migration out of the African forests to the grasslands of the East African plains; 60,000 years ago humans left Africa and migrated all over the planet, and their descendants have been migrating ever since. In 1620, one in ten people in the Netherlands was foreign born; in cities such as Amsterdam this could be as many as one in four. In 1855 half the population of the city of New York were immigrants. The populations of North America are almost completely made up of migrants or their descendants.

Although some figures will have changed since she wrote in 1990, few have put it better than Lynn Pan:

Migration is the great travel saga of all time. People have always moved to find land and work; and to flee from war, famine and oppression. They have also, at times, been forcibly relocated; for several centuries people were transported into slavery from one part of the world to another by Europe's imperial powers, and when the slaves were freed a substitute was found in Indian and Chinese indentured labour. The scale of the population relocations flowing from voluntary movement, mass transportation or expulsion has been immense. Since 1800 no fewer than twenty-eight million people have migrated to America. The First World War displaced nearly a million people; the Second World War, forty-five million. Today about four to five million foreign workers from South and Southeast Asia live abroad, supplying cheap labour to the world's richer countries. And an estimated twelve million refugees, a third of them in Africa, are awaiting resettlement or seeking asylum (375).

In the next chapter we will look at forcible displacement; here we will consider those who have left their homes voluntarily – although conditions in their own countries might not have given them much choice.

In the last couple of centuries, with the development of faster and safer modes of transport, the extent of movement has accelerated sharply. Lynn Pan is herself part of the Chinese diaspora.

I was born in Shanghai, was made an émigré by the terror campaigns of the Chinese Communist Party, and was educated, in a manner of speaking, in Hong Kong, British North Borneo and England, where I eventually established a base. I was going to say "made my home", but that would suggest I had put down roots, whereas I often get the feeling when I'm in England that my real life lies elsewhere, though exactly where it lies it is difficult to say (Pan, xi).

Lynn subsequently went back to China, and has now been living in Shanghai for over ten years.

Some migration has been deliberately engineered to suit receiving countries – importing cheap labour from poorer countries. Following a poster campaign in the West Indies advertising for jobs in the UK, shiploads of mainly ex-servicemen began to arrive. The arrival in 1948 of the first ship, the *Windrush*, heralded a new era in Britain, an era of multiculturalism. Very few of the new arrivals intended to stay more than a few years, and, having been invited to the "mother country", they expected to be welcomed. But, as other visitors to our shores have found, what they encountered was very different: exclusion from much of the social and economic life of the country and blatant discrimination. Letters home were either relentlessly cheerful or revealed the darker reality of, for instance, seeking accommodation and finding notices such as, "No blacks, no dogs." Homesickness was countered by lack of money and, despite the problems, many people stayed. The result has been a powerful enrichment of the society to which they came.

As Mike Phillips writes on the BBC history website:

Caribbeans began to participate in institutions to which they did have access: trade unions, local councils, and professional and staff associations. The people of the Windrush, their children and grandchildren have played a vital role in creating a new concept of what it means to be British. To be British in the present day implies a person who might have their origins in Africa, the Caribbean, China, India, Greece, Turkey or anywhere else in the spectrum of nations.

The now-familiar debate about identity and citizenship was sparked off when the first Caribbeans stepped off the Windrush... In a sense the journey of the Windrush has never ended.

On 22 June 2008, the 60th anniversary of the arrival of the *Windrush* was celebrated extensively in London and elsewhere in the UK. A number of church services were held and a procession wove its way from Clapham North deep shelter, where the new arrivals had been temporarily housed, to the Clapham Common bandstand for celebratory speeches, music and drama. Veterans and descendents of the *Windrush* generation made a special journey up the Thames, on the "Windrush Ferry".

The poet, James Berry, talks of being brought up in Jamaica to feel special because they were British, learning English songs, attending a Church of England church, being part of a greater whole. When they arrived in this country, he and his family had to adjust to the fact that the British did not see it like that. But James Berry can see the contribution that he and his fellow-immigrants have made. In his poem, "A greater oneness", he gives us his vision of a people coming together as one:

> walking with multifarious faces,
> with love, with peace, with essential growing.

> ...Man – I goin to Englan
> to help speed up Englan
> into a greater oneness
> with an ever growing humanity.

There are millions of migrants living temporarily or permanently in other countries, often for economic reasons. Although their services are often needed in a host nation where there is a shortage of labour or an ageing population, they are frequently viewed with suspicion. Life can be a struggle financially too: most are on low pay and are sending much of their earnings home to support the family. It is estimated that the amount of money sent home by those living abroad is bigger than the amount of aid given by rich nations to developing countries. Joanna is just one of that vast number of migrants working abroad to help their relatives at home. She is Brazilian, 29, and working in London as a cleaner. She works seven days a week and cannot afford to do less, because of the low pay and the money she sends her family. Four of those days are at a pub, starting at 6am. She never stops for a coffee when she is cleaning, and was surprised when one of her employers gave her an Easter egg. She expects nothing; cleaning is her life. She has no time to find a partner, or for anything other than sleep.

For the millions round the world who have overstayed their visas or entered the country illegally, life is even tougher. With no employment or citizen rights or access to public services, their pay and conditions can be "subject to sudden changes", and they live in a state of continual anxiety, "with an extra pair of eyes", as one man put it. In the UK the number of illegal workers is thought to be over half a million. In recognition both of their contribution to the community in doing jobs few others would tackle, and the innate injustice of a system that leaves people in a ghost life often for years, all the candidates of the 2008 London mayoral election called for an illegal immigration amnesty.

In the States, there are some 11½ million illegal migrants, many of Latino origin. In 2006 mass rallies were staged across the country to complain about proposed new tough immigration measures. Immigrants boycotted work or school and avoided spending money as a way of showing their worth to the economy. "Everyone's an immigrant here," said a Puerto Rican-born doorman in a Manhattan hotel, at the time. "The only real American is the Indian."

Moving to a new country is not easy, even if it is legally and by choice. In the East End of London, a focus for new migrants over the centuries, a social inclusion project was recently opened to provide services for young women who have been in the country less than a year. After eight months it already had over a hundred women signed up for English and IT classes and the personal support to enable them to feel at home in their new country. The women are encouraged to register to vote and to open bank accounts.

At the launch I spoke to three young Bangladeshi women, who have moved to the UK because of marriage. All have attended English classes at the centre, and spoke warmly of the support they have been given. Two of them have been in the UK for only a year; it was surprising to hear how much at home they feel. All would say that the UK was home: Noorjahan, because her husband is here. Nasima tellingly said, "I have to think of this as home or how would I live comfortably here? I try to accept this as home, like Bangladesh." Unlike the other two, and unusually for her culture, she lives alone with her husband, who has no family in this country, having come over on a work permit five years ago. She felt lonely to begin with, but is getting used to it.

The other two live in large households: with in-laws and their children, one in a household of eight, the other nine. Yes, they do feel cramped in three- and four-bedroom houses, though they enjoy living in big family groups. Houses in Britain, built for the usual smaller size of British families, are "small" compared to those they are used to.

Nasima said that they were safer in this country, and the other two agreed. In Bangladesh it is not considered safe to go out alone as a woman, "because of the poverty and muggings". Here, they enjoy their freedom, walking, or travelling by bus. Nasima emphasised that there were lots of opportunities to build their lives as women. Next year they will go to the local FE college to improve their English. All were traditionally dressed, heads covered, Noorjahan in a sari, and they lead traditional lives. All three do the cooking and cleaning for their households, though Shahriya, who has been here for two and a half years, said that she shares the work with her mother-in-law, with whom she gets on. "She is a good person." Asked if they would have felt as much at home in an area with fewer people from Bangladesh, they looked doubtful, but obviously found it hard to imagine.

These are women with optimism and energy, who, despite

missing their country of birth, have settled very quickly, and look for opportunities to expand their horizons. Statistically, Bangladeshis like these women are among those living in the most overcrowded conditions in the country. But perception is moulded by expectation, and these women are content. Noorjahan said that if she died she was sure her husband would bury her here. Her sister-in-law had died five years ago and was buried here. "And would you be happy about that?" She nodded.

The Pakistani-born writer, Nadeem Aslam, came to Britain as a teenager. While expressing his own gratitude for the opportunities he has been given, he recognises that others who come to these shores have not been as fortunate. Those working in occupations that expose them to drunken racist comments will have had a very different experience from his own, and will have passed their views on to their children. Add to that the fact that these young people are plunged into a society where activities forbidden to them as Muslims are commonplace – pre-marital sex, music, alcohol and women with exposed heads. It is no wonder, he says, that they are alienated and confused. Less than half British Pakistanis aged 18 to 24 feel that Britain is their country.

Tony and Peter are South African. Despite having lived in England for many years, Tony said, "I've never felt completely at home in this country. Belonging enough not to be excluded but not finally belonging. I quite like standing on the outside." As a novelist, he is content to be an observer. Peter feels differently: "The older I get, the more of an outsider I feel in England, and standing on the outside – but I don't like it."

Virginia was also born in South Africa and spent her first five years there. She first went back when she was well into adulthood, and remembers feeling "this overwhelming sense of home – just getting off the plane, I felt it".

Mary Jo, who was born in the USA and has lived in England for many years, says that in the UK she is told she has an

American accent; in the US that she has an English one. She feels between two worlds, however benign.

Carol is also between two worlds, but has felt torn for many years. An Englishwoman in her sixties, she has lived in Dublin for much of her adult life and her son, now in his twenties, was born and brought up there. "Home? It's being without a state. I don't belong anywhere. My relationship with England has fragmented as a result of my family relationships. When I'm here [in England], I'm in bits, because I want to belong here and I don't. I'm a traveller. I understand how asylum seekers feel. I think it's time I applied for membership of my Quaker meeting; not so much a spiritual decision, as the need to belong somewhere."

Harvey says that he has lived in a lot of places, and doesn't deny the "at-homeness" of any of them. Home is "where I feel I slot in at any given time." It's being affirmed, accepted and comfortable. In a place or a relationship that feels right. He has, he says, been at home in many places, and rejoices in his good fortune.

Sometimes a sense of belonging takes people completely by surprise. Kimmett, an American, was never particularly keen on travel and didn't speak other languages. When, at the age of 23, the opportunity for a student trip arose, he chose to go to England. The result was astonishing. "I hit the tarmac and thought, 'I've come home'. It was an eye-opening experience," he said, "to be at home for the first time in my life." In the US, he felt he was always having to adjust to fit in, and now he was fitting in. "It was a question of my and England's warts fitting. That's why I live here. By accident I came on a student abroad trip – and came home."

Sometimes the familiarity of a place is overwhelming, even if one has never knowingly been there. A sense of déjà vu – something glimpsed in a dream, maybe, or a memory rooted in the genes. Jo talks of driving in France, and feeling it is her country, her home. Warren, who believes profoundly in the reality of past lives, visited the mediaeval Spanish city of Toledo as a student, and wrote, "As I walked the streets it was as familiar to me as London, by that time I knew that my Jewish ancestors had been expelled from Spain in 1492 but the full significance of my strong memory of the city only became apparent when I started to study and practise Kaballah [Jewish mysticism]."

9

Broken circles

Displacement

Exile is an ancient form of punishment. Being cast out, transported, sent away, in most cases never to return, was a powerful infliction of pain for often trivial wrongdoing. But it has also been used on a vast scale to exert power and to drive out difference. In 1838 the US Indian Removal Act forced the exile of Cherokees, one of the "five civilised tribes", from Georgia to Oklahoma. During that terrible winter some four thousand Cherokees died on the thousand-mile march. In the twentieth century, nearly thirty million people were sent to labour camps within the USSR. Today, slavery, although no longer legal, is even more widespread than before the abolition of the transatlantic slave trade. It snatches up the lives of millions and puts them to work in carpet factories in India, cocoa plantations in Africa, domestic labour in the UK and the USA, and the sex industry all over the world.

Force may take the form not of kidnapping but of the imposition of conditions of such danger that inhabitants have no choice but to flee. Leaving one's home and country is the last resort in situations of extreme danger in war, oppression or abuse. The definition of a refugee according to Article 1 of the 1951 Refugee Convention, is someone with "a well-founded fear of persecution on account of race, religion, nationality, membership in a particular social group, or political opinion".

No one wants to be a refugee. Those of us who live settled lives, who have not lived through war or oppression, can have little idea of the turmoil, the violent uprooting, displacement causes. Life is uncertain: home even more so. Cut off from family and friends, divorced from house and country, home becomes a concept of memory and dreams rather than any present reality.

There are refugees on both sides of my family, one immediate, the other many centuries ago. My father's family was of Huguenot descent. In the late seventeenth century, the family escaped religious persecution in France and came, as paupers, to live in the East End of London, for hundreds of years and thousands of refugees, the arrival point in the country. When I was working in the East End, in the late 1990s, giving loans to mostly refugee women to start businesses, I received a letter from a previously unknown relation, living in Washington DC. He had researched earlier generations of the family than we had previously known about, and eventually sent us a book about the family. When it arrived, I discovered that in about 1700 a pair of brothers arrived in the country, destitute, came to live in the very streets I was working in, and were given money to start a new business. After three hundred years, I felt as if I was paying it back.

Ten years later, I discovered the existence of 19 Princelet Street, a museum of migration, housed in an old Huguenot building. Although it was on the At Risk register, and mostly closed through lack of funding, it was going to be open during Refugee Week, in June 2008. I found an old building, beautifully unrestored, with open brick walls and stone slabs on the floor, a testimony to the waves of migration that have passed through the area. Formerly owned by a master weaver called Peter Abraham Ogier, the building also houses a Victorian synagogue, built in 1869 by Jewish émigrés, and now the last of its kind remaining in London.

A three-minute video shows local schoolchildren, of Bangladeshi and Indian origin, telling a Jewish folk tale and singing a Jewish song. A group of new immigrants honouring the culture of a former group is a beautiful example of acceptance and integration. A small girl who had come to this country only a short time before sits among old brown suitcases and introduces the programme. A small group of boys act out some of the action. "That's me," said one of the museum volunteers, pointing to the screen, "seven years ago". Santokh was born in a nearby street and, like the rest of those children, at that time considered himself simply as a Londoner.

At the end of the exhibition, visitors are asked to fill in a card asking: which was the last member of your family to come from another country? What are your roots? What is your identity? With consideration, these are profound questions. Santokh now says his roots are "Indian Cockney". London is his home; the cultural aspect comes from India. He said it took time to understand that he was anything other than English, and that it was important to recognise his roots, and what previous generations had endured for him to be there. His granddad, a builder, came over in 1949 to get a job and send money home. Fifty people shared a house, with half working by day and half by night, sharing the beds. His father, "a punk rocker", nonetheless had an arranged marriage, as he himself will. A third-generation Briton, he still values the traditions of his inheritance.

My connection with the place did not end there. When I got home, I looked at the book of my father's family history. There, on the page, was the name of Ogier. My family had married into the family that owned the museum. I was thunderstruck. The reasons for writing this book were more profound than I knew. I could almost believe something I had read a few days before, that my ancestors were walking with me.

My mother, Genia, is 93, a Russian Jew who left Russia on the back of a hay cart with her mother and brother at the age of five. They left her father for dead, although they learnt later that he was in a Bolshevik prison. One day, before they left, men arrived at the house. Baby Genia was in a cot. One pointed a gun at Genia's mother, and asked her where her husband was. "Go ahead," said my grandmother, "shoot." The other man gestured at the cot, and shook his head.

My mother has no memory of feeling at home in Russia, a place of anti-semitism; only of profound relief at leaving. She went to school in Latvia, where her grandparents lived, but never liked the country. It was only when they arrived in Switzerland that she could relax: a place of safety, "a democratic country", in which she grew up and for which she has a profound affection and respect. As a child Genia never had a home, felt only tolerated in the home of relations; moved countries, languages, schools. She often felt more at home with friends than with her family. "They were good to me. I was happy; we had a lot in common." She arrived in this country in 1946, married to an Englishman, no question of her admittance. She has lived in many countries, feels she is adaptable, embraces different cultures, though some more readily than others.

Her sense of home? "One's own house and home. To be born and brought up in a country that is one's own. Another country is never quite the same." As a foreigner, she hasn't "really felt regarded as part of this country. My loyalties are entirely here, but I have recently felt less at home; it's crept up on me because of all the other nationalities that have come to live here."

There are few people so exercised about the advent of a new wave of refugees as refugees from a past generation. My mother's last comment sheds a little light on why that is. Those outside a country have a more fixed idea of its identity. I remember the very pronounced ideas about Britain that I came across when travelling round the world. People from other countries were attached to a pastoral idyll where cricket is played on the village lawn, or convinced that London is continually immersed in a Dickensian smog. They did not really want to hear about a rich multi-cultural community: they wanted their picture of Britain to stay the same. I think the same may be true of some who settle in this country. On arrival it can take time to settle in: to match the country you arrive in with the country of your imaginings. One young Bulgarian woman, steeped in English literature, found it hard to come to terms with the twentieth-century reality. Once established, coming to terms with change may be even more difficult. People know why they have come here, why they wanted this to be their home. Change is not welcome. For someone born here, the (maybe unconscious) sense of belonging is more established. Members of the indigenous population may feel threatened by competition for housing or jobs, but their sense of the identity of the country is less undermined by the advent of people from elsewhere.

Scattered round the world are vast refugee camps; the dwelling places of people displaced from their own countries by war, oppression or fear of persecution. Near the town of Tindrouf in Algeria are four refugee camps the size of towns, established when Morocco invaded Western Sahara, a tiny but mineral-rich country in West Africa. It had once been under Spanish colonial rule, but in 1975 the International Court of Justice recognised the Saharawis' right to self-determination and Spain agreed to organise a referendum. But the following month, over 300,000 Moroccans marched into the territory. In the settlement known as the Madrid Agreement, Spain agreed to end colonial rule, Morocco acquired two-thirds in the north of the country, and Mauritania the remaining third.

Hundreds of thousands of Saharawis fled to nearby countries. More than thirty years later, they are still there. In December 2000 when Meg spent a week in one of the camps as a volunteer, there were some 200,000 people living in a mixture of tents and mud huts. They had built the houses themselves, along with clinics and schools. This was always to be a "temporary" abode until they went home, but they recognised that in the meantime they would have to provide the necessities of life. Some of the population had been nomadic, but most had come from a settled community in a prosperous area. Western Sahara is coastal and boasts good fishing. Now, the refugee community depends on charitable giving from Spain and other North African countries. Water container lorries arrive on a daily basis, there being no running water. The camp is run as a collective, with chickens and market gardens. Most of the population is Muslim, with a few Christians, but they are together in solidarity.

By 2000 a whole generation had grown up in the camp, with no knowledge of their own country. Talk of going to an idealised "home" was frequent. Meg felt their problems would begin when they went back – if they did. Her own feeling is that they never will; they are too few to have any power. Already many of the young men have disappeared; some who are enabled to go to university in other countries never return. She feels that the Saharawis will simply disappear as a people. Morocco's position is that their land was always part of Morocco until Spain took it over, that there is no such country as Western Sahara. Like the 2,000 inhabitants of the Chagos islands, evicted in the 1960s by the British to make way for an American airbase on the atoll of Diego Garcia, there is little hope that they will be allowed to return home.

The fact that these camps are in Algeria is not surprising. Contrary to popular belief, it is developing countries, with the majority of their own people living in extreme poverty, which are host to the largest number of refugees. Iran and Pakistan host twice as many refugees as do all the countries of Western Europe combined. In 1999 Africa, with 12% of the world's population, had received nearly half of its displaced people. People leaving extreme hardship, war or abuse will move either to the nearest country that will accept them, in the hopes of a quick return, or to countries where there are family ties. The view of many countries that they are "overwhelmed" with refugees, that people fleeing their country, for whatever reason, head for rich countries in the West, is not borne out by the facts. According to the charity, Refugee Action, the UK, for instance, hosts only 3% of world's refugees.

Western countries have a distorted view of their own generosity. Until recently I believed the commonly held myth of Britain's "proud history" in opening its doors to those in danger, that it is only recently that we have closed our hearts and doors. But I discovered that in the Middle Ages foreigners had to pay fees before they were allowed to settle in a town and had to pay another fee before they were allowed to work in certain professions. Some areas discriminated against Catholics, others against Protestants, and almost all discriminated against Jews.

At the international conference held at Evian in 1938, as one government representative after another stood up to explain why their own economic difficulties precluded them from taking Jews fleeing Nazi Germany, Britain was no exception. Exhibitions in London's migration museum bear witness to our reluctance over the centuries to give hospitality to those in need.

But the last few decades have seen an increasingly draconian attitude to those seeking asylum. There has developed a culture of disbelief that has led to acute xenophobia in some quarters, and increased levels of destitution among asylum seekers. Although the word "bogus" is no longer attached to tabloid headlines in the UK, hostile and inaccurate reporting continues to create a climate of misinformation and fear.

A report by the Council of Europe has attributed blame for the increase in racism in the UK to increasingly restrictive asylum and immigration laws. According to the report, the frequent changes to legislation designed to deter people from seeking asylum in the UK have had a central role in the general negative climate. The report states:

Many politicians have contributed to, or at least not adequately prevented, public debate taking on an increasingly intolerant line, with at times racist and xenophobic overtones.

Public statements have tended to depict asylum seekers... explicitly or by inference, as a threat... politicians should not only avoid promoting the general assumption that most asylum claimants are not genuine, but also the vilification of those who are considered by the authorities not to have valid asylum claims.

"I have never felt British. I have always felt foreign." "I don't feel I am rooted anywhere, and that's painful, actually."

These are the voices not of present-day asylum seekers, but of daughters of two of the 85,000 Jews who fled to Britain to escape the Holocaust. Although my mother's journey was different, I am also a second-generation Holocaust survivor, and it echoes my experience – although I don't feel it to be painful. Maybe I did as a child; I don't remember.

But I do remember that as I child I never felt that I belonged. With a foreign mother and then when I was five a father who was diagnosed schizophrenic, we didn't seem to fit in. So I made an asset of our difference. That sense of not belonging continued even through being head girl, captain of the hockey team, all that. Maybe I was conformist because I thought it would help me belong, although I didn't want to, consciously. When I started an independent literary agency, it took me six years to join the professional association. I still have the letter that welcomes me "at last"! I have always felt an outsider.

But, said a friend wisely, have you ever met anyone who thought they did belong, that they were an "insider"? Maybe it is always others who are insiders, who belong, never ourselves. For most, including myself, it is not a serious problem – I have generally led a happy life – but what is serious is a tendency to bolster ourselves, as we did, by feeling superior to those who are more visibly "different". I have come to recognise that the way society excludes some groups of people is not only a fear of the difference of others, it's a fear of our own difference.

And for those groups, the sense of exclusion is a reality that eats into their lives, prevents them from engaging in society. It is not just a sense of being different, though that is true too: it is of being treated differently – with less kindness, justice and equality.

In the UK, asylum seekers are expressly excluded from the inclusion agenda. Government policy has actively *increased* exclusion in areas considered key for other groups (employment, income and housing). While an asylum claim is being investigated – and this could take several years – a claimant is entitled to £5 a day, in food vouchers, not cash. If an asylum seeker receives a negative decision on their claim, their accommodation and cash support are withdrawn within 21 days. The Home Office expects refused asylum seekers to leave the country, but many are unable or unwilling to return to countries where they have suffered persecution and where they fear retaliation. They remain in the UK without statutory support or the legal right to work, and lack the means to meet their basic needs.

The Independent Asylum Commission, led by a former senior judge, reported in 2008 that the treatment of some asylum seekers was a shameful blemish on the UK's international reputation. Policymakers were at times using "indefensible" threats of destitution to try to force some asylum seekers to leave the UK. "We heard worrying stories about the conditions being experienced by some asylum seekers, in particular the scale of the destitution," Sir John Waite told the BBC. "The picture that emerged was one of people struggling to live." The hearings had also come across torture victims and pregnant women being fast-tracked through the system, despite official guidelines saying this should not happen. Overall, the report said that the treatment of asylum seekers fell "seriously below the standards to be expected of a humane and civilised society".

In 2007 an investigation into the position of asylum seekers in one UK city was held by the Joseph Rowntree Charitable Trust.

The report was disturbing. Even more disturbing were the findings of the follow-up report in 2008:

The number of refused asylum seekers living destitute in Leeds has increased by 180% over the last 18 months: the problem is chronic, with more vulnerable people lacking either the safety net of support or the right to work. More have been destitute for longer, and more children are involved.

"Imagine", writes Mark Haddon in the new newspaper, *The New Londoners,*

what it must be like to live this kind of life, to leave everything behind, your job, your family, your home. To travel to Stuttgart in the back of a truck. Or Oslo. Or Rotterdam. Any place where you don't speak the language. You have no friends. You sleep in the street, or share a house with strangers who speak yet another language. Imagine living on £35 of Asda vouchers a week. Imagine not being able to see your family. Then ask yourself what kind of experience would make this kind of life preferable to going home.

Wezenet keeps herself and her children by working two days a week as an advisor at a refugee drop-in centre. The rest of the time she runs a small charity as a volunteer to support other African women asylum seekers. She told me her story.

I left Eritrea when I was nearly 14 years of age. When me and my friends were on our way to school, Ethiopian soldiers tried to take us to their camp. When we refused to go with them they started beating us. We rather die than go with them. They left scars in our body and hate in our hearts. My friends then decided to join the Eritrean freedom fighters, but

I left to the Sudan with my other friends and neighbours. I left my parents back in Eritrea, it was really painful experience to be separated from my family.

On our way to Sudan we were supported by a lady who was taking her daughter and her son whose husband was in Saudi Arabia. (I also had my sister living in Saudi Arabia.) She took seven of us children from the neighborhood to Sudan, we all stayed together until we found our ways. We had nothing; I had no money or food. This woman had two children of her own, yet when it came to food, she spread it out in the middle of us – I remember a big platter of rice – and told us to share, to help ourselves. I was amazed, and watched her. She always made sure everyone else had something before she ate. I asked her: "You have your own children; why do you share the food with us?" She said, "I want you to remember this plate, and how we all share it. When you are rich, make sure you share with others. We are all one." She has been a huge influence on me.

It was a terrible journey: we hid during the day, with bombs going overhead all the time – once a bomb dropped when we were making bread, the dough was splattered all over the place. We had nothing to eat for two days. At night we would travel through the bush, with snakes and everything. It was awful.

In Saudi I met my husband. I married when I was 20. My husband was a great fighter fighting for the Eritrean Liberation front. He was a great fighter who always loved his country. When I had two children I came to England, he could not get a visa. I waited for him for ten years, after he came to England, he got cancer, and after five years living with us, he died. He was only 43 when he died. Because of the culture I had to take his body back to Eritrea. His family was so pleased to have his body. I believe that my husband would have wanted it, although he hadn't said anything to me. It was horrible experience. His family said they didn't need to mourn now they had it, and thanked me for bringing it. I thought he's dead, what does he care? My son asked me if I wanted to be buried in Eritrea. Absolutely not! If I die, I am happy for my body to be buried where I die, anywhere.

A few months after we spoke, Wezenet was able to take her children back to Eritrea for a month's holiday – the first time she had been back since taking her husband's body for burial. Despite not wanting to be buried there, it was significant that she spoke of "going home".

March 08. In a scruffy room in a North London church five women are having an English lesson, run by Wezenet's charity: how to ask questions, the use of "can" or "could"; the difficulty of the change in pronoun between asking "Could I have some milk" and answering "Yes, you can." These are women who have been in the country between five and eight years: four Eritrean, one Moroccan in a djellabah, all originally asylum seekers. Language is their greatest obstacle – and they find the weather difficult. Asked what they think of the English (and I begged them to be honest), they all said "nice people, helpful". Then one added, "just don't ask them for money." Laughing agreement from round the room, then one added, "Yes, don't ask an English person for money, just ask for directions"!

These light-hearted comments hide backgrounds of pain and suffering, and acute uncertainty about their future. Most had come to England alone. Moura, a teacher who had her own college in Morocco, had come to England with her six-year old son, leaving her husband and two small daughters behind. In England her son developed eye cancer and lost his sight. He is now 13, with artificial eyes.

Anita has children, but she lost track of them during the war in Eritrea, and has no idea where they are. She herself has been in the UK for eight years. For seven years she received Social

Services support, then one year from the National Asylum Support Service (NASS). Last October she was given exceptional leave to remain, but only for five years, and they haven't sent the right documents. Without documents she has no right to anything. So, since October too she has been homeless, and without any money for the last two months. She is 65; the small charity has applied successfully for pension credit, but this too is waiting for the documents. In the meantime she asks for money from friends: £2 here, £5 there. The church, she says, has been wonderful, has helped her since 2002, encouraged her, prayed for her, given her emotional support – opened their door to her. The church is her "address"; all her belongings are there. She is Christian Orthodox; the church is Catholic, but there is no problem. "There is only one God." This is caught up by the others. Some Eritreans are Orthodox; others Muslim, but there is no divide. In Eritrea no one asks what religion you are. "There's only one God," the others agree.

Anna too was homeless when she first moved to London, first staying with friends, and eventually on the street. "But it was the summer," she said. "I was lucky." She moved into a hostel and is now housed in a temporary housing association flat. She does not know how long she can stay there. Six months ago she got a British passport, after nearly eight years in the country. She is now at college, studying.

A fourth woman, Eva, told me she had been receiving NASS support and housing, but then pushed a letter across the table, and burst into tears. NASS has held a review of her case, and decided she is no longer entitled to support. No explanation is given. She has had to leave her flat, and has come to the charity for help. Wezenet thinks that it is because the Home Office do not recognize the Eritrean Liberation Front, to which Eva belonged, or believe that she will be in danger if she returns. In order to progress her case she will have to bring new evidence, but after years in this country, she has no idea what evidence she could bring. If they accept new evidence, it will be like a new case, and she will be allowed £30-£35 per week from NASS until the case is sorted out one way or the other.

Home? "It's life," said one of the women. "Yes, life," another echoed, then made a dramatic gesture of cutting her throat. "If you have no home you have no life; if someone cuts your throat you have no life."

I asked the teacher, who came to England from Trinidad at the age of five, what she thought was "home". "A house, a family, children and parents. Where you go to (or hope you can go to) when you're stressed." Then she said "Love", and there were murmurs of assent from round the table.

"And Eritrea," I asked the women. "How do you feel about that?"

"Wherever we go, still we miss our country. We feel we belong to that place, even if we are happy and healthy. Something is missing. Our real home. If there was peace, we would go there." All except Wezenet agreed that they would want to be buried there.

For Moura there is a happy ending. She is now reconciled with her husband and her other children, all of whom are now in the UK. She is trying to get a job.

Exile is an uncertain place where identity and belonging are in suspension. For many refugees, "home has become an elusive idea, haunting and dangerous. Home was what defined them, and what they were forced to abandon. The image is always that of abandonment, their own and that of others. And home, in a place of exile, rarely exists." And the experience of return is not always like the dream. One of the people to whom Caroline Moorehead talked said he belonged neither to one place nor another. "Even if I go back to Eritrea now, I will not belong there. I will be strange to people, and they will be strange to me... Wherever I am, for the rest of my life, I will never be entirely at home again" (Moorehead, 234). Doubly excluded.

> Suicides are not unusual among asylum-seekers in Britain.
> Not all are committed by men and women who have reached
> the end of the legal line and are facing imminent deportation,
> for the life of an asylum-seeker is precarious, confusing, beset
> by contradictions and reversals, subject to sudden uprooting
> and dispersal, all of it for the most part conducted in a foreign
> language. For some the waiting and uncertainty are already
> too much. For others, the loneliness is more than can be borne.
> When, early in July 2003, a young Iranian used a knife to try
> to hack himself to pieces... he left a note: "You have to kill
> yourself in this country," he had written in large scrawled
> letters, "to prove that you would be killed in your own
> country" (*ibid.*,134).

The gradual integration of generations of migrants across the
world has produced a rich mix of cultures. It is now questionable
whether this will continue as

> governments, having allowed asylum-seekers to become
> scapegoats, have effectively marginalised them and made it
> harder for them to integrate. Though refugee protection,
> drawing on many different strands of international law, is
> now embedded in human-rights and humanitarian treaties
> and agreements, restriction, not generosity, has become the
> order of the day (*ibid.*, 35).

When he was Secretary-General of the UN, Kofi Annan reminded
us that politicians have a choice to make. They can either

> embrace the potential that migrants and refugees represent, or
> use them as political scapegoats. Immigrants and refugees
> should not be seen as a burden. Those who risk their lives and

those of their families are often those with the greatest ambition to make a better life for themselves and they are willing to work for it.

There are chinks of light. In the UK, faith groups are buying food vouchers off asylum seekers in large quantities some individual churches to the extent of £1,000 per month – to enable more flexibility in spending: on phoning relations, for instance, or on fares. Another chink is the launch of "City of Sanctuary" in a number of British cities: a grass roots programme in which individuals and small groups from churches, schools or clubs pledge hospitality and inclusiveness in their daily lives. These are small subversions of an iniquitous system: small examples of the invaluable role that individuals and the voluntary sector can perform in "breaking down differences, recognising connectedness, bringing different realities into contact, working towards a single 'real world' in which we can all feel at home" (Best & Hussey, 161).

Another example is Spare Room, a national organisation set up in 1996 as a concern of two London Quakers. When the law changed so that anyone applying for asylum from within Britain would not be eligible for accommodation, they realised that thousands would be made homeless, and wanted to do something about it. Since then, the organisation has found a home for some 32 people from many countries. Spare Room matches up refused migrants without recourse to public funds with hosts who have a spare room and are happy to host someone for a few days, weeks, or even years. Now an ecumenical organisation, Spare Room is run as a co-operative. Clients are referred by other organisations, or come by word of mouth; there is always a shortage of hosts, particularly in London, where most of the guests want to stay. Paul's is a typical story. Already living in the East End of London, with a network of friends, attending college, and volunteering for a local refugee agency, he was sent to Luton, then to Portsmouth – people in his position have no choice about where they are sent to live. He was raided in the middle of the night and sent into detention. It appeared later that there had been an administrative error. No one had taken note that he had been sent to Portsmouth; he was arrested for having failed to sign on in Luton. Spare Room intervened and got him released. After ten years in this country, he still has no status. He now informally tutors students and belongs to the local Anglican Church. He has settled again, and regards his Spare Room placement as home.

Chris is one of the founders of Spare Room. He and his wife have hosted four guests in their East End home: from Albania, Zimbabwe and Uganda. His current guest has been with them for three years and chaired the last meeting of Spare Room. Asked why he started the programme, Chris says:

> I have a calling to provide shelter for those who have none. As a teenager I put up a homeless man who was singing in the streets – much to the distress of my mother. "When I was homeless, you gave me shelter": Jesus' challenge. Basic Christianity.

Detention

Each year in the UK 30,000 people seeking asylum are detained. People are taken into detention often after many years in the country, with children established at local schools, English their only language; the family part of the community.

Trudie came to the UK in 2001 from Uganda when she was 17 years old and applied for asylum the next day. She writes:

> I had to flee Uganda because my father wanted me to marry a man from the Sebei culture who was twice my age and would have forced me to undergo female genital mutilation. When I refused, my father started abusing me; beating me and locking

me up in the house. He raped me and as a result I gave birth to a baby girl who he wanted to kill.

My claim for asylum was refused when I turned 18; even though the immigration judge believed how I had been persecuted, he still refused my claim.

In 2005, when my daughter was 5 years old and my son was 1 year old, we were detained at Yarl's Wood detention centre. My children were very scared and kept asking me why we were locked up, what had we done wrong, and if we had committed any crime.

Eventually, we were released, but in 2006 I was re-detained – this time without my children, who were put into foster care. After ten days, I was taken to the airport by "immigration escorts" to be removed to Uganda, and they brought my children. The escorts abused and threatened me. I was handcuffed in front of my children who were so scared, terrified and they were in tears.

And the pilot came and told them they weren't taking me, he told them to get me off the flight. They started abusing me, asking "Why did you try to resist? Why didn't you behave? Why, you black idiot? I couldn't believe they treated me like that. So then we went back to Yarl's Wood.

Since Trudie arrived in this country she has studied Health and Social Care; her children are at school; the family has integrated well into the community. She is a regular church-goer and has volunteered with a number of organisations to support fellow asylum seekers. Recently she completed a human rights advocacy course. Despite making a home here, she and her children are still in danger of deportation.

There are plans to prevent the embarrassment of forcible deportation on public flights. "Asylum Airlines" would be a private airline exclusively running deportation flights. The planned flights would have a human rights representative on board. Costs would be reduced by cutting the number of private security officers that are currently required to accompany those who are deported. Instead, the specially modified asylum airline planes would have seats with built-in straps and restraining equipment for "disruptive" passengers. Those who continue to resist their forced removal will be taken to padded rooms built into the aircraft.

Some Gatwick detainees are tagged. One man was deported, leaving his wife and children behind. When they arrived at the country of destination, he was not accepted, and sent back. On the way, his papers were lost. So he has none, possibly for the rest of his life. He is too scared to ask for any, in case he is again sent away. In another case a woman was deported without her children, who were then adopted.

About two hundred children are taken into detention in the UK each year: subject to indefinite detention without trial. Who has the power to take up their cause? There is a clause in the 1989 Children's Act specifically excluding the children of asylum seekers from its protection. The Children's Commissioner is independent but cannot take up individual cases. There are guards even in children's wards in hospital. A child at Yarl's Wood detention centre asked: "Why am I in prison for things I didn't do?"

In 2007 there was a record number of "enforced removals", often at dawn. One woman from Yarl's Wood talked of being forced on to a plane with her children, the guard's elbows digging into her back, and a whispered "If you don't get on this plane, I'll break your arms." Only following regulations. Where has such brutality by "ordinary Britons" come from?

Segregation

One of the most cynical uses of the word "home" was in the use of "homelands" under the South African system of apartheid ("separateness"). The "home" of black people was no longer to be in their own country. South African blacks were stripped of their citizenship, legally becoming citizens of one of ten, theoretically sovereign, *bantustans* (homelands). The government created the homelands out of the territory of Black Reserves founded during the British Empire period. These reserves were akin to the US Indian Reservations, Canadian First Nation reserves, or Australian aboriginal reserves. Many black South Africans, however, never resided in these "homelands".

The aim was to ensure whites became the demographic majority within South Africa by having all ten *bantustans* choose "independence". Not all the homelands chose to become self-governing, as they understood that, while they would have absolutely no place in South Africa, they would still be controlled by the apartheid government (in spite of their "independence").

The search for a homeland has been at the centre of Jewish identity for millennia. The festival of Sukkot, also known as the Feast of Tabernacles, requires Jews to build a temporary hut with a roof of branches and leaves, and stay there for eight days, open to the sky and the providence of God, as a reminder that they were refugees in an alien land. The creation of Israel was an answer to the pain of exile and, most recently, to the horrors of the Holocaust in which one out of every three Jews in the world was killed. It was not an answer, of course, for the Arabs displaced by its creation, still less for those remaining, and sharing the land.

This is not the place to go into the complexities of the history of Palestine and Israel, nor the rights and wrongs of the political situation. As Arab and Jewish peace-workers within Israel and outside it have recognised, people of both races live in fear and have suffered terrible losses of friends and family. I wish only to mark the lack of freedom and daily restrictions that constrain life and work for Palestinians; the inequities that mark the daily reality of a people segregated within their home country.

According to the United Nations there are over 500 physical obstacles restricting the movement of Palestinians from one town or village to the next within the West Bank. Israel has imposed these restrictions in order to protect Israeli settlers who have been settled in the West Bank against international humanitarian law. Palestinians have to apply for permits from the Israeli authorities to cross the checkpoints and gates and many are refused them. In 2004 the International Court of Justice gave an advisory opinion, which stated that the "separation barrier" built on occupied land is illegal and it violates the Palestinians' right to freedom of movement as well as their right to health, education and work. In July 2008 a delegation of prominent South Africans, including several Jews, was invited by Israeli human rights organisations to visit Israel and the Occupied Territories. Themselves subject for many years to the oppressive regime of apartheid, the South Africans were appalled at what they found in the Israeli-controlled heart of Hebron. According to the *Independent*'s report, "800 settlers now live there, and segregation has seen the closure of nearly 3,000 Palestinian businesses and housing units." Palestinian cars are not allowed to drive in this area. Nozizwe Madlala-Routledge, former deputy health minister of South Africa, said, "Even with the system of permits, even with the limits of movement to South Africa, we never had as much restriction on movement as I see for the people here."

The Ecumenical Accompaniment Programme in Palestine and Israel (EAPPI) provides protection by presence, supports Israeli and Palestinian peace activists and advocates for an end to the occupation. Since 2002, hundreds of volunteers have been sent out from fourteen countries to stand at checkpoints that dissect the West Bank, and at gates at the "separation barrier", to try to reduce the harassment or abuse of Palestinian civilians or to help them gain access to their land. They also provide protection to vulnerable communities at risk of violence from hardline Israeli settlers.

A man in the Hebron area whose house was bulldozed to the ground cried: "Do I have another forty years to do this again? This is my father's land, my grandfather's land. Israel is killing the homes inside people."

Segregation on the scale of the examples of apartheid and Israel may not exist in many countries, but few have the right to be complacent. It is not so long since racial segregation was a legal fact of life in the USA; there are few countries which represent an equal "home" to all its inhabitants. As we saw in Chapter 6, in most of our countries there are inner borders.

If we accept that the world is home to every human being, that the boundaries we have created are artificial divisions in the human race; if we accept that the suffering of any one person diminishes us, what can we do to lessen that suffering? Inner and outer borders are created by possessiveness and greed. With global communication, we cannot fail to be aware, to be overwhelmed by the pain, poverty and injustice of the world. The inequality, both within nations and between them, is an ever-widening gap. Can we in Western nations constrain our desire for more and more? Acquisition is not fulfilling but addictive; our yearning is without end. Can we bring back that infinite yearning, that yearning for the infinite, from its material expression to its proper spiritual dimension?

Gandhi emphasised the role of simplicity in effecting change: "Live simply, that others may simply live." Can we change our view of "progress" as quantity? Can we move towards not more but less? It is not enough to wish for others what we have ourselves – it has been said that if all six billion people on the planet had a material standard of living like that of the UK, we would need three planets; for that of the USA, we would need seven. So if the world is to be equitable, we have to be content with less, with enough for what we actually need. Then there will be enough food, fuel, land and housing for all. It is in small matters, in the everyday, that we can express our love for others, prove our kinship. As well as by pressing for political change to redress the inequities of our markets, we ourselves can become examples of caring living.

That remarkable young Canadian woman, Severn Suzuki, addressing the UN in 1992, talked of how we in the North are afraid to share, afraid to let go of some of our wealth. "Why", she asked, "why are we who have everything still so greedy?"

Borders are enforced by ignorance and fear. Only when we distance ourselves, fail to perceive another's reality, fail to recognise the humanity of a fellow human being, can we ill-treat or exclude him, and consolidate our fear in repressive legislation.

An astronaut wrote of encircling the earth:

You look down there and you can't imagine how many borders and boundaries you cross again and again and again, and you don't even see them. There you are – hundreds of people in the Mid-East killing each other over some imaginary line that you're not even aware of, that you can't see. And from where you see it, the thing is a whole, and it's so beautiful (Katz *et al.*, 11).

Let us break down the borders and boundaries in our own lives and see the beauty of the whole. Let us dream of "a world without walls".

10

The harmony of O
Our sacred home

sacred. safe. nourishing. playful palette. quiet. animals. plant beings. ritual. Charlie. music. study. growth. color. richness. always something to be done, always something to do. books. art. labyrinth. healing. friends. debates. coffee, strong and aromatic in the morning. 14 year old compost, rich and rolling with earthworms. Mississippi Kites circling in the summer, Red Tail Hawks circling in the winter. something always in bloom. s.h.m.i.l.y. (see how much I love you). work.

These are off the top of my head when I think of "home" this morning.

Also,

mesas. sage. high desert. rabbits. vultures floating in the sky. azure blue sky. red and magenta mesas. apple green cottonwood trees. filling my lungs with pure, brilliant, air. the sun, caressing my skin, lightening my hair, purifying my soul. ancient. each moment a new discovery of delight as the sun and clouds play across the land. seeing the "ancient ones" silhouetted in the cliffs, breathing their wisdom down the canyons. "feeling" the great cougar watching. following the wing-beat of the pinon jays. peace radiating to and from my core. listening to the landscape with every fiber of my being. These are the two "homes" I live in. One here in Baton Rouge. One in New Mexico.

Robin

Always living close to nature I learnt many lessons from the design of God's creations. Very rarely do we find the square or the rectangle but very often the circle is used. The straight

line is rare, but the graceful curve is frequently seen...
Furthermore, I have found the answer to many spatial and
planning problems by using the circle and the curve instead of
the square and the straight line – and building becomes much
more fun with the circle! (http://lauriebaker.net/work)

Looking around us, the softness of the curve or circle is always
evident: in the shape of an egg or nest, the centre of a flower,
ripples of water in a pond, circles at the heart of a tree, marking
its age, how the sun and moon appear to us – and our own planet.
The circle is characteristic of the indivisible, self-sustaining
character of nature itself.

Not that we often see it like that. Even when we are concerned
with the environment and the ecological impact of our behaviour,
we rarely make the connection or understand our own
connection to the object of our study. According to the Oxford
English Dictionary, ecology is the study of "the mutual relations
of organisms with their environment". We are one of those
organisms: we are part of the object of our study; it is our relation
with our environment that we are looking at. As Martin Buber
says, "We live our lives inscrutably included within the
streaming mutual life of the universe" (20). Matthew Fox's
definition of ecology is "the study of our home". The derivation
of the word ecology, after all, is the Greek *oikos*, meaning home.

It is possible that in the centuries before Copernicus, when the
view of mankind was of a universe centred on the earth, when it
was believed that everything revolved round us, that there was a
stronger sense of being at home in the universe. When we were at
the centre, maybe there was less of a psychological need to create
a separate home of our own. However that might be, particularly
in societies focused primarily on the individual, we are less
aware of our natural interconnections, and have a need to find
something bigger than ourselves.

Belonging to the Universe is a remarkable conversation between two Benedictine monks and a physicist/systems analyst, bringing together the wisdom of religious experience and scientific exploration. Mystic experiences in all faiths of the wholeness, the interconnectedness, of the universe have been confirmed in recent years by scientific research. In 2008 tiny fragments that could be the precursors to genetic material were found in fragments of meteorites from Space. It was further evidence that the death of stars has contributed to the birth of our planet, and of life itself. When stars explode, they shower forth a vast array of precious metals. The carbon in our bodies, the minerals in our rocks, say the scientists, are made from star dust. "To let us live," a speaker on BBC radio's *Cosmic Quest* said, "millions of stars have had to die." Their sacrifice. It is easy to romanticise "nature", but we are all aware that it is also "red in tooth and claw". It is in the nature of different species to feed on each other. A tough ruthless world, but also one in which sacrifice plays its part.

The mutuality, the interdependence, of species has long been evident in every tiny detail of the lives of millions of plants and animals. Insects feed on nectar and carry pollen from one flower to another. The decline of the kittiwake population in the Scottish islands of the Orkneys is driven by changes in the availability of the fish that these birds depend on. We need plants in order to breathe in; they need us to breathe out.

And of course our interconnectedness does not end with our own planet. We are completely reliant on our local star, the sun, which has the power over us of life and death. We belong to something on an unimaginably vast scale: one trillion galaxies with an eighteen-billion-year history.

The more and more deeply one sinks into our cosmic existence the more fully one realises the truth that there does not exist an inside and an outside cosmos but rather one cosmos: we are in the cosmos and the cosmos is in us... All things are interrelated because all things are microcosms of a macrocosm (Fox, 69).

Some intimations of the scale are given to those who travel in space:

Now he looks back and sees the Earth not as something big, where he can see the beautiful details, but now he sees the Earth as a small thing out there. And the contrast between that bright blue and white Christmas tree ornament and the black sky, that infinite universe, really comes through, and the size of it, the significance of it. It is so small and so fragile and such a precious little spot, that little blue and white thing that is everything that means anything to you (Katz *et al.*, 12).

The Earth was small, light blue, and so touchingly alone, our home that must be defended like a holy relic. The Earth was absolutely round. I believe I never knew what the word round meant until I saw Earth from space (Aleksei Leonov in Vardey, 538).

We take our planet for granted in a most breathtaking way. We travel to distant lands, have seen the earth from the moon. But even here, where we are now, the life and beauty and infinite variety of our earth is open to us. Even in a city we are given the different shape and shade of leaves, the colour of petals; moss growing on a wall; a flower thrusting up from a crack in the pavement. Life is bursting out everywhere with insatiable energy; in the park, water-birds in their variety of shape and size and habit: the elegant necks of swans and stately herons, geese, ducks, coots swimming, ducking, playing, washing, sleeping. The squawks, chirrups, clucks and pure-throated song. The variety of flight, the glide, flap, wing beat with legs dangling, tucked or stretched behind. The scale and scope, the sheer diversity of the created world is the context of our life. Awe and wonder and celebration of our earthly home are a natural response. We have been given life. It behoves us to take notice!

And more than take notice; to cherish the Earth as the source of life, nurturing and sustaining humankind and the rest of creation, fostering growth and fertility. Instead, in our arrogance, we ill-treat the animal kingdom with medical experiments, squeeze chickens into batteries, pin butterflies to a board. Albeit illegally, cock-fights and dog fights continue. Even individuals who would try to avoid swatting a fly or treading on an ant conduct an unthinking lifestyle that endangers other forms of life. We pollute the earth, the air, the oceans and even Space; we endanger the lives and health of human beings, especially in the poorer areas of the world, and the existence of other animal species, and plants. We are fouling our nest.

There may be few that believe in a literal version of the biblical account of the creation of the world in seven days, but the commandment in Genesis 1.28 that man should "have dominion over the fish in the sea, and over the fowl of the air, and over the cattle, and over the earth, and over every creeping thing that creepeth upon the earth" has stuck fast in human consciousness, and still holds sway. We are a species of explorers and endowed with intellectual curiosity, but too often that curiosity leads to colonisation and exploitation. We cannot, it seems, discover anything without wanting to use it, subdue it, take control. We plant flags on mountains, and at the North Pole; the battle for the sea-beds of the world has intensified as we reach out for the financial rewards of their rich mineral reserves.

Mao Tse-tung inherited Confucius' view that life was a struggle of man against nature, and that man must conquer it. Mao built a number of dams to prove it, including the Three Gorges Dam on the Yangtze river, causing a great deal of environmental damage, and displacing millions of people. And he is not alone. In 2000, the World Commission on Dams estimated that dam projects in India and China accounted for the displacement of at least 29 million people. After adding in figures from Africa, the Americas, and Europe, "40 million constitutes a conservative estimate". And that is not to count the environmental damage. One small part of that is the effect on the water itself, and on the life it supports. Water renews its oxygen by the bubbling movement of its rivers. Dammed rivers cannot do so.

The essence of vitality for any ecosystem is complexity and balance. In a free-flowing mountain river, the physical, chemical, and biological conditions that constitute habitat for a single living creature change drastically over short distances in all directions – upstream, downstream, shallower, deeper, in front of a rock, behind it, under it. This heterogeneity makes for spectacular diversity of species... And that diversity in its turn makes for great complexity of interlocking relationships, great richness of life, and balance (David Quammen in Vardey, 662).

We live on the surface of the earth; we walk on it, drive on it, and build on it. The other day, suddenly aware of a huge new vista of sky that had opened up near where I live in the heart of a big city, I realised that a building the size of a street block had been demolished, and caught a glimpse, before a new building arose, of how the earth is without our man-made structures. As Alain de Botton says:

We owe it to the fields that our houses will not be the inferiors of the virgin land they have replaced. We owe it to the worms and the trees that the buildings we cover them with will stand as promises of the highest and most intelligent kinds of happiness (267).

We grow our food in and on the earth. We also pour into it

pesticides and herbicides, and experiment with genetically modified crops. We dig into it, tunnel beneath it and bury millions of tons of non-biodegradable rubbish into it. We exploit its riches while knowing little, and heeding less, of what lies beneath the earth's crust. That vast unmapped area of the earth's core, living evidence of the young days of our planet.

There is another life beneath the oceans. Snorkelling or diving reveals a world of tranquillity and beauty: the habitat of thousands of species of fish and sea animals, each with its own unique organism, all with different feeding habits and forms of communication and reproduction. I remember as a child crossing the English Channel on a boat, and being horrified to see one of the ship's officers throwing an enormous bin full of rubbish into the sea – visible, physical pollution of the ocean on a daily basis. No one questioned it and no one knows the extent of the damage we have done to that habitat and those creatures. Objects from plastic bags to condoms and shampoo bottles are washed up on beaches all over the world; fish are found to have swallowed all sorts of alien objects, and birds are frequently damaged by leakage of oil from passing ships.

In 2004, two oceanographers from the British Antarctic Survey completed a study of plastic dispersal in the Atlantic that spanned both hemispheres. "Remote oceanic islands", the study showed, "may have similar levels of debris to those adjacent to heavily industrialized coasts." Even on the shores of Spitsbergen Island in the Arctic, the survey found on average a plastic item every five metres. The director of a wildlife recovery centre in the Canary Islands said that 75% of the sea turtles that they receive have been hurt because of man's activities. "We see turtles damaged by hooks, nets, pollution, oil and plastic bags. Turtles damaged by boats are the worst to recover. We try to patch up their shells with fibreglass, but survival rates are low." Despite the Ocean Dumping Reform Act, the US still releases more than 850 billion gallons of untreated sewage and storm runoff every year, according to a 2004 Environmental Protection Agency report. Even in the early 1970s, the diver and environmentalist, Jacques-Yves Cousteau, found that overfishing, human and industrial pollution and unrestrained "development" of its shores had reduced the marine life of the Mediterranean by 30 to 40%. From the Gulf of Mexico to the Black Sea, the number of "dead zones" where the levels of oxygen are barely able to support marine life has doubled every ten years since the 1960s – due, it seems, to a run-off polluted with nitrogen-rich crop fertiliser.

Air pollution is becoming one of the biggest dangers for the future of the planet, causing increases in allergies, especially hay fever, and premature deaths of humans as well as damaging flora and fauna through acid rain. According to the Worldwatch Institute,

more than a billion people – one-fifth of all humanity – live in communities that do not meet World Health Organization air quality standards. In greater Athens, the number of deaths rises six fold on heavily polluted days. Mexico City has been declared a hardship post for diplomats because of its unhealthy air. In Bombay, simply breathing is equivalent to smoking half a pack of cigarettes a day. In the U.S., air pollution causes as many as 50,000 deaths per year.

Today, even Space is littered with our waste: non-functional satellites and booster rockets, explosion fragments, paint flakes, dust, rubbish and human waste thrown out by space programmes. It is estimated that there are more than 600,000 objects larger than 1 cm in orbit. If worry is expressed, it tends to be about possible danger to functioning satellites, not about our effect on the purity of our environment.

We are the only species that produces waste (other than excrement) – and we produce it in massive quantities. It is estimated that in the UK we throw away a third of the food we buy. Our acquisitive and throw-away culture demands that we buy the newest model and dispose of our old machines – TVs, computers, mobile phones and audio equipment – and, increasingly, it is not only far cheaper to replace than to mend, it is impossible to find the parts for something to be mended. When a hinge broke on my oven door, I could find no one who would or could fix it. After months of propping it shut with a broom handle, I had to buy a new oven. In Egypt or India I know that I could have had it fixed within days. In poor societies, people make the most of everything, stripping down equipment to find the useful and recyclable parts. Unfortunately much of the equipment that we dump on foreign shores has toxic components. We are, as one commentator said of e waste, the millions of computers finding their way to developing countries, "poisoning the poor".

It took a long time for me to have any understanding of what some utterances of an Old Testament God might mean. Like many, my response to such passages as "visiting the iniquities of the fathers upon the children, unto the third and fourth generation" was one of revulsion. However, it came to me a few years ago that what is being described is not the punitive judgement of a autocratic old man pointing a finger at erring humankind, but a statement of fact. Of cause and effect. The effect of our behaviour on the next generations is the reality; it is what happens. The impact is inherent in the act. Maybe in this way I can find a way of coming to terms with the concept of karma.

And so it is with our treatment of the planet. If we have any sense of the life-force as a connecting principle, that which binds together the whole of creation, then we can see the effect of our denial of that connection in what happens: in floods, melting ice-caps, tsunamis and earthquakes. Only when our own physical or economic wellbeing is threatened, it seems, do we begin to take notice. T Boone Pickens' conversion to wind power in Texas is not to do with the effects of oil on the environment, but on its cost. "We're paying $700 bn a year for foreign oil," he said. "It's breaking us a nation" (the *Independent*, 12 July 08). The voice of the man who started Mesa Petroleum appeals to American car-owners worried about the rapidly increasing cost of filling up their tanks.

We need to modify our behaviour not for our own gain and protection, but because of a sense of responsibility to the rest of creation. We need to move from an arrogant "dominion" over the rest of creation to acknowledging our place as one among equals. To remember that we tread on the same land, we share each other's breath, and that there is nothing called waste in nature.

In 1992 a young woman called Severn Suzuki, representing a group of twelve and thirteen year olds from Canada called Environmental Children's Organisation (ECO), raised the money to go to Rio de Janeiro to address the United Nations. She spoke of her fear of losing her future; she spoke for all future generations and all the starving children in the world, and all the animals dying across the world "because they have nowhere else to go". She told of her dream of seeing "great herds of wild animals, jungles and rain forests full of birds and butterflies" but wondered if they would still be there for her children to see. She talked of the ozone layer, polluted air and fish with cancers and told the UN representatives, the adults of the world, "If you don't know how to fix it, please stop breaking it…"

We are all part of a family, 5 billion strong, in fact 30 million species strong, and borders and governments will never change that… We are all in this together and should act as one single world working towards one single goal.

Some fifteen years later, Severn has modified her approach. As the www.celsias.com website reports, she continues to be active about raising awareness of the environment, but rather than trying to shame people into seeing sense, she has learned that slow, quiet solutions may be more realistic. She is currently pursuing a master's degree in ethnoecology, a discipline "...which draws on perspectives from the natural world, traditional beliefs, science, social trends and the politics of interests on Canada's West Coast." As part of her studies, Severn is analyzing how some communities have successfully survived for thousands of years by using their natural resources sustainably. She looks to ancient traditions as models for those in Western society making short-sighted decisions that will deplete the Earth for future generations.

There are signs that climate change, holes in the ozone layer and the melting of Arctic ice are bringing us to our senses. As we become more aware of the effects nature and man have on each other, we appear to be moving towards a more co-operative view. We need to move still further to an understanding of our shared creatureliness; co-creation. Stewardship is a word often used to express our responsibility to the earth, but even stewardship implies that we are in charge. All we can do, perhaps, is heal some of the damage that we have done, and guard against doing more.

We do not own the earth. We cannot actually own land, though we think we do. The inhabitants of countries like Mongolia where there is no private land live in recognition of that, as do the indigenous peoples of the world. The earth is precious and, in a desperate irony, it is those who treasure it most who have had it taken away. White people on the whole see the value of land in monetary terms, and take it because they want its oil and minerals. We take, we rob the earth of its riches without consideration of the cost. We don't know how to live in harmony with the earth. Those who do have had it taken from them.

I don't think the dominant society... understand that to live as a human being is to live as a sacred being and that everything on this planet is sacred. The earth could live without human beings but we think that we have this value and that somehow control this whole thing, but we're nothing more than a parasite on this planet and this earth is starting to react to that... Do Indian people understand that? Yes they do. That's part of the consciousness of planning for the recovery of the Indian people and may be what it takes to bring Indians back into the situation where they are able to live in harmony with the earth again (Chapman, 127).

During my time on Pine Ridge Native American reservation, I caught a glimpse both of the deprivation and the spiritual richness of its inhabitants. Deprived of the Black Hills, the land on which buffalo roam, the Oglalas are detached from their spiritual heritage. All animals are sacred, but for this tribe the buffalo has particular significance. A source of meat, skin for clothing and hooves for glue, connection with this animal is a celebration of abundance and gratitude for the richness of life. It is a point of spiritual significance to honour any animal which is killed by using every part of the body. Waste is a desecration of a sacrificed life.

I was privileged to be present at a blessing by the local medicine man of the land on which a house was to be built. The occasion was a solemn and powerful one, though I did not understand the details of the ceremony. Subsequently a Cherokee pipe-holder explained some of the ways in which a house is blessed and protected. "In my lineage," she says,

we usually begin with the East, then move in a clockwise direction. We call in the essence of each direction. East – new beginnings, movement, the rising sun, the Eagle; South – the teacher, Coyote, joyful, playfulness, the child; West –

Grandmother Medicine Bear, the healer, the wisdom of our ancestors, death; North – White Buffalo, the intellect, wisdom, strength.

"A gross oversimplification," she says, but it gives the idea. Living in Louisiana, the heart of hurricane country, she explained how they were protected in recent storms:

One of the things I do, and teach, is to place a protective circle of corn meal all around our property. This is a powerful, yet simple thing to do, and is key to why our property continues to be "injury free" during such events.

Corn meal is one of the sacred plants/herbs. It is key to the survival of "The People", and is fundamental to the lives of the people of the South West. We use it in a sacred, humble way to give thanks to All That Is, all that surrounds us and infuses us in this world and others. For a protection, we pour, by hand, a contiguous stream of corn meal around our entire property line. We also bless, honor, and protect each tree in the same way. We walk the land in a sun-wise direction, and we make sure the line is not broken. We also walk the footprint of our house, creating circles within circles of protection on our land.

The result of this is that where ever we have placed the sacred corn meal, there has been NO damage.

This is one form of house/home blessing that I know from long experience works on all levels. It protects from home invasions, storm damage, and major problems of all sorts.

Other things that we do for home blessings and protections are to use sage and sweetgrass. We burn the sage, walking from room to room in a sun-wise/clock-wise direction, making sure to address each window and frame, door and frame, beneath beds and furniture, and into each closet. We allow the sage to burn as it will, taking care to not put it out regardless of the volume of smoke that arises. When this process is complete, we then follow with sweetgrass. The sage purifies and releases old, stagnant, dense energies that don't serve us. The sweetgrass invites the benevolent spirits and energies into our space and home.

In addition, often, we will incorporate the use of crystals and gem stones in this blessing/healing process. These energies and sacred ancient beings can be so helpful in healing and protecting a home. Sometimes these are buried, offered to the earth around a home. Sometimes they are placed within the home.

Tobacco, sage, sweetgrass, cedar, and corn meal are all used in some fashion for a healing and blessing of a home.

This is very specific: physical, and literally grounded. John Todd of the New Alchemy Institute, who says "I've been in love with the Earth's living mantle since I was a small child", conducted an experiment with some friends. In their attempt to "create a commune where we could come into harmony with the earth", he and his colleagues realised that they needed to understand what was going on in their piece of land. Each person had to study one aspect of the place and share it with the others. "One after another we began to become sensitive to this particular place and it changed us; I don't think any of us has ever been the same since." One realisation was that in order to grasp anything a reduction in scale was necessary: "a reduction of the scale of our being to the point that we can grasp tangible wholes" (Katz *et al.*, 177, 178). In order to understand our planet home, we need to notice what is going on, to observe the details of other life, and respect them.

We have so much to learn from the natural world. Think, for instance, of the cooperativeness of geese. As each goose flaps its wings, it creates an uplift for the bird following. By flying in a 'V' formation, the whole flock adds 71% more to its flying range than if each bird flew alone. When the lead goose tires, it rotates back into the formation and another goose flies at the point position. In formation, the geese from behind honk to encourage those in front to keep up their speed. Whenever a goose is sick or wounded, two geese drop out of formation to help and protect it. They stay with it until it heals or dies.

"Sustainability" is a word much bandied about, without much understanding of its meaning. The 1987 UN Bruntland Report defines it as "meeting the needs of the present generation without compromising the ability of future generations to meet their own needs". Our responsibility to the future has been well understood by Native Americans who, in taking every important decision, consider its impact on the seventh generation. Neale Donald Walsche considers that "your heirs stand beside you, watching your decisions on their behalf" (298).

As the mother of small children, Helena in Canada is all too conscious of her heirs, and wonders how to raise them so that they will connect with the issue. In expressing her deep anguish about "the threat to this home called the earth", she likens it to the nuclear wake-up call of the 1960s.

At every level – internationally, nationally, locally, and personally – we are beginning to consider what we can do. And, yes, as individuals, it is possible in this as in other areas, to make a difference.

Nearly half of the UK's energy consumption comes from the ways in which our millions of buildings are lit, heated and used. It is not surprising that attention is increasingly being given to how that consumption can be lessened. Katie told me of how she lives:

We have installed a rainwater saving system that we use to wash our clothes and flush the loo. Generally the green bit comes in our ethos for using recycled materials from skips, buy and sell ads, friends' networks, etc. We also try to make our own where possible – for example cutting down on food miles and packaging by making wine, yoghurt and herbal preparations.

A house in south London, heralded as "London's first retro-eco home" was the first private home in London to export solar electricity from the roof – to London Electricity. Its hot water is heated by a solar water heating system powered by a solar pump; the WC is supplied by a rain harvester, and the wind turbine installed in it enabled the owner to become London Energy's first ever domestic wind electricity supplier. The house is heated by a wood burner powered by waste wood, and the heat is spread through the house by a little eco-fan. In 2007 it finally became not only a zero carbon home but by a modest 116 Kg became carbon negative. It sold more green electricity from its solar electric panels to the national grid than it imported fossil fuels. If all this sounds completely daunting, a visit to the charming little two-storey house showed it all to be small-scale, domestic, and within the bounds of possibility – a life of simplicity. Time-consuming, yes, but maybe we need to take more time to acknowledge what and how much we are using: to be mindful of the daily impact of our lives.

At the Ideal Home exhibition in 2008 there was a queue for the Eco house: a carbon neutral house built out of a flat-pack kit. Features included a roof-top allotment, insulation made of sheep's wool and hemp wool, shutters for warmth and security, a suspended floor to house pipes, etc, and afford some protection against flooding. Large water tanks, no foundations, but piles, solar heating with access to the National Grid, were some of the features – and people were interested. Pieces about "greening" our houses appear regularly in British newspapers. The tide has definitely changed – not just out of duty, it seems, but from an innate sense that this is the right way to go. Green is no longer a fringe notion; it has become "cool".

At the migration museum in Spitalfields, London, a schoolgirl – perhaps ten years old – paused when filling in the card about her roots and identity. Her identity?

"Well," said a helpful museum volunteer, "a girl?"

"No, it doesn't matter to me if I am male or female."

"A member of the human race?"

"No, that doesn't matter to me."

"What does matter to you?"

"Nature."

"And how do you fit in? Are you a part of nature?"

The girl nodded, "Yes, that's it." And she wrote down "A part of nature."

Now I am at home, this is my home. And I belong. I belong to all the animals, to the plants. And belonging means I am at home with them, I am responsible for them and to them…We all belong together in the great cosmic universe (Capra *et al.*, 15).

11

The O of completeness

Coming home

I. To self

Existence is an intricately interconnected web of relationships. We share the breath of life and thus we are connected. Whether we are rich or poor, black or white, young or old, humans or animals, fish or fowl, trees or rocks, everything is sustained by the same air, the same sunshine, the same water, the same soil. There are no boundaries, no separation, no division, no duality; it is all the dance of eternal life where spirit and matter dance together... The process of the universe is embedded in the life support system of mutuality (Kumar).

Yes, the same universe is home to all of us, but home to each in a unique way. No two people will perceive the world in the same way. The "at-homeness" of each will be subtly different. The less a way of life expresses the inner person, the more important it will seem to have a geographical home to bring one back to self. As Alain de Botton says,

What we call a home is merely any place that succeeds in making more consistently available to us the important truths which the wider world ignores, or which our distracted and irresolute selves have trouble holding on to (Smolan and Erwitt, quoted in the *Independent* 7 June 2008).

In one sense, the whole of life can be seen as a search for home, an identity, a journey to be at home in one's own skin. For some there will be a geographic rootedness, a clear understanding of belonging. But many – and increasingly in a fragmented world – will be torn, restless, finding it hard to find a context in which the self can be at home. Others will explore what Gandhi called "the horizontal diversity of the world" or will find that no geographical context is necessary: "rooted" as Simone Weil wrote, "in the absence of a place".

I used to be a visitor at Pentonville prison in London: a vast container of 1200 or so men, most of whom are being held there for a short time, waiting for a court judgement, or on their way to a longer-term jail. A harsh, inhospitable place, full of comings and goings, with no time to form friendships or feel part of a community. I visited Ben one day. We sat on the steps of the landing, there being no other easy place to meet. Ben was a Buddhist, and he pronounced himself to be utterly at home. His cell was his space; he did not feel constrained. Despite not being free in any physical sense – he was locked in, not free to leave and was subject to being told what to do for much of the day – he had made even that inhospitable place his own. He felt free.

How do we come home to self? How can we feel at home in our own presence, without worrying about the value of our belongings, without a continual need for distraction, or a puffing up in status, bank account or grandeur of surroundings? Sometimes, as we have seen, it can simply come upon us, take us by surprise, but for a more lasting state, some work is usually necessary.

Will feels he has different levels and layers of self:

At the moment I am searching for the home where I am at ease with me as a soft baby. I feel I have created a home for myself. In the last eight years I have culturally excavated home. I have reconnected with my ancestors and the land of my parents' birth [Jamaica]. And, beyond that, Africa. A heritage home – I have accomplished that to a degree. There's a real sense of belonging.

But he feels that there is a gap between that real sense of self and a sense of belonging in the family he grew up with. "I don't yield, I don't have that relationship with my family of birth." And that has implications for his relationship with his partner and four children. "The same places I am unsurrendered, unforgiving – they're there in my own family life. So how can I be at home with my own family when I am not at home with my family of birth?"

It's a life's work, first understanding, then coming to terms with, the different layers of our belonging. All human beings live with "baggage". We won't necessarily "get over" all our sense of pain and loss, but the jagged bits will become less sharp as we accept them as part of the totality of our life's experience. No one said it was easy. Only when we have, to some degree, made peace with the different aspects of how we relate in the world, will we come home.

I am good at shutting doors on the past, closing compartments of my life that no longer seem relevant or might be painful. I don't think it's necessary to penetrate deeply into all of these rooms, but peace demands a certain integration of where we have come from with where we are now.

Inner hospitality

Coming to terms with where we are now calls us to work on what John O'Donohue calls inner hospitality. We need to work on self-acceptance, on recognising, reaching for and expanding the sense of a world within, our unique world from which we approach the outer. Once we accept ourselves, "can live with" ourselves as we are, we will not feel the need to compete, to project, to show off or to battle with others. Once we trust ourselves, we will be able to trust others, to breach the walls of fear, hostility and defensiveness with which we surround ourselves.

And we will not put ourselves down. In the Alternatives to Violence Project, the first building block is affirmation of self and others; a guideline for all workshops is that there shall be no put-downs of others – or of self. The latter is much more common. Lack of self-esteem is the starting point for most anti-social and dysfunctional behaviour.

In the Jewish and Christian religions we are bidden to "love your neighbour as yourself". Some of us will find loving ourselves the harder task. How to achieve this wondrous state? My own experience is that the journey mirrors that which we take in relating to others. The journey, it seems to me, begins with compassion. While being all too aware of our faults, we can suspend our judgmental tendencies, and regard ourselves with gentle kindness.

From compassion, we can move to understanding, acceptance and, finally, trust.

So much of what we do in life is running away. Rather than staying in the home of ourselves, we do anything to escape. We distract ourselves. We run to the past and the future. The past has gone; the future does not yet exist. The past may never have been how you remember it, and the imagined future may never come to pass. Only by being in this present reality can we be said to be at home.

Rather than doing something, we need to stop. Stop our busyness, our filling of every moment with activities, noise, company, worry about the past or anxiety about the future or what is taking place elsewhere. Stop, and let the peace creep in. Stop, and let the body relax, pay attention to the breath, the sounds around us: where we are now.

If we take time to do this on a regular basis, this peace will become a part of our lives. There will then grow a space in which the inner voice can be heard, a leading to what is true for each of us as unique individuals with failings and flaws, but also with boundless potential. Courses, workshops and books can support us on the way, but there is no substitute for allowing ourselves to be. Giving ourselves permission.

But we are not alone. In reaching within, ironically, we will come upon the place which connects with others: the place of Spirit that connects with Spirit in other people and the rest of creation that bridges diversity to reach the One. It is from that still place, that place of truth, that we most truly relate to others, a place which others perceive as something solid to which they themselves can relate. Just as there are some buildings, some houses, that have a positive ambience, a "good feel", so we have all met people who radiate a grace-filled state of being. Even with no speech, it draws us. Inner acceptance is inviting to others. As Henri Nouwen says: "We are always in search of a community that can offer us a sense of belonging, but it is important to realise that being together in one place, one house, one city or one country is only secondary to the fulfilment of our legitimate desire" (33). If we are at home, it allows others to be so too. If we are always "out", there is nowhere for others to visit. Friendship and community are, first of all, inner qualities.

I find it easy to be addicted to superficial routines: playing patience, a particular radio programme, checking emails on my computer: a need to know that other people are in touch. External stimulus. When I am away from such routines – and I make a point of travelling without a radio or a computer or a pack of cards – I am liberated. Without distractions I have to allow myself to pass through a boredom threshold, to allow myself to be "bored" in order to move into another state, a state well described by the Trappist monk, Thomas Merton:

Contemplative life must provide an area, a space of liberty, of silence, in which possibilities are allowed to surface, and new choices – beyond routine choices – become manifest. It should create a new experience of time, not as stopgap, stillness, but as *temps vierge* – not a blank to be filled in or an untouched space to be conquered and violated, but a space which can enjoy its own potentialities and hopes – and its own presence to itself. One's <u>own</u> time. But not dominated by one's own ego and its demands. Hence open to others – <u>compassionate</u> time, rooted in the sense of common illusion, and in criticism of it (*The Asian Journey of Thomas Merton*, New York: New Directions, 1975: 117).

A few years ago I spent a month in the Outer Hebrides, first in a croft B&B, then in a little house by the sea. I walked and thought and prayed and cried: I worked on my dependencies. I was recovering from the break-up of an important relationship, and was in spiritual preparation for what I knew would be a challenging time on a Native American reservation. It was a time, as Henri Nouwen says, of moving from loneliness to solitude. That time changed me. I have no doubt that that period of my life and the months that followed it in a little house by the sea on the south-west coast of England, settled me more in my solitary, independent self.

When asked about "home", quite a few people made no mention of a house, a country, or an external place of any kind. Responses included:

"It's in the body, not in a place"

"It's where I lay my head. It goes with me"

"Home is what the whole of life is about"

"It's every minute of every day that I live. People not bricks and mortar. Home is wherever I am."

"'Home is where the heart is, where I hang my hat'. It's wherever I am. I can be hitchhiking along the road, and that's home for the moment. The environment that I inhabit, where I feel safe and comfortable. It belongs to me. I belong to me."

"My home is within me. All I need is within me. I have all the resources I need: I just have to find them."

"Peace in one's soul. Yes, that's it, to be at peace in one's soul."

"Interestingly," said Frances, "for me it's the activities that take me out of myself: driving alone, drawing, painting, reading, being asleep. When I feel most at home is when I forget myself most." This is echoed by the Benedictine, David Steindl-Rast, when he writes about the paradoxes of even minor peak experiences: of feeling most ourselves when lost in an experience, of feeling most at one with all when we are alone.

But for many the sense of self needs a secure physical context: "something more interior, but the outside needs to be safe and peaceful" or "a balance of shelter, of familiarity, one's own-ness, and one's selfness".

One woman said how her son hated being asked "Do you live at home?" "Of course I do," he said, "by definition!"

II. To faith

I had a spontaneous awakening and the awakening was I became one with the cosmos or entered into what I believe Eckhart Tolle calls the present moment or the presence and in that present, all of my former ideas... dropped away and all of a sudden, I realized that I was home. I actually was reflecting on this question, where is home and what is home? And it came up to me, of course, that I am always at home and at home is right here, right now and it is not out there someplace else, a physical place or a physical house, and in that awakening, everything became very simple and very obvious and very clear. All of my troubles, all my sorrows disappeared or vanished.

My fears, my suffering, everything went and I experienced what you might call being one with God, one with the universe, one with the all, the whole. It was all about somehow finding and discovering, in myself, a place that was clear and spacious and where the self was no longer a problem. The self was no longer present (Genpo Roshi, www.masteringthepowerofnow.com).

Coming home to self will, for many, be part of a spiritual journey. An inner voice, but part too of something beyond us. God within and without.

I don't remember my first Quaker Meeting. What I do remember, after a darkly troubled time, is finding peace. And, as the weeks went on and I read about a way of life that had little to do with any previous understanding of religion, I realised that I had come home. Such a discovery is almost a cliché of the spiritual life. In listening to men and women of many faiths, I have heard many talk of "coming home". And that "home" can be somewhere that is found for the first time.

So, what does it mean?

In my case it meant an invitation – indeed, a requirement – to be myself, to be true to an inner voice, the voice of the Spirit. It meant listening, letting go of the need to control, and allowing my life to be guided. Guidance for me generally comes through other people, and often takes the form of synchronicity. Many have testified to the importance of seeming coincidences in their lives, inklings of interconnectedness and unity, glimpses of a greater whole. When several synchronicities – a phone call, a piece in the newspaper, a chance meeting – confirm a path, a direction, that for me is clear guidance.

Coming home also meant a sense of belonging. When I had been attending a Quaker meeting for about six months, our meeting ran an away weekend. I remember my disdain at the theme of the weekend: "Belonging? I've never wanted to belong. Don't believe in it." By the end of a weekend of sleeping under the same roof as about 30 others, eating together, talking, walking and worshipping, I sat on the Sunday morning with my eyes closed, mentally going round the circle of Friends. I realised I knew everyone in the room. A powerful sense of belonging overwhelmed me. I realised not only that I did belong, but that I had always wanted to. All those years of feeling an outsider, different, separate – making a virtue of that difference had been a cover-up for the pain of isolation. As is so often the case, I had denied what I most desired. It was at that point that I decided to apply to join the Religious Society of Friends.

But my sense of belonging was to something greater than that group of people, a religion, a label of any kind. It was the beginning of an understanding of my place in the world, of interconnectedness, a process that opened my heart to the love at the centre of existence.

I was introduced, recently, to a mantra:

Breathe in to "I am".
Breathe out to "Thank you".

I might add:
Breathe in to "Life (or Love or God) is".
Breathe out to "Thank you".

The authors of *Belonging to the Universe* affirm my experience: "Faith is a courageous trust in belonging... In our great moments we experience that belonging." They go further: "God is the great 'Yes' to belonging that holds everything there is together" (Capra *et al.*, 24,108).

Neale Donald Walsche writes emphatically: "The destination is the same for all of us. We are all on a journey Home, and we shall not fail to arrive there. God will not allow it" (x).

I am not comfortable with this certainty: it is too reminiscent of a concrete understanding of "heaven", a perfect home that awaits us elsewhere. Neither does his analogy appeal. The spiritual path and journey are well-worn metaphors for our spiritual quest, but in fact this emphasis on the linear is not helpful. Isn't the seeking rather for depth, fullness, living with increased awareness and amplitude? To give in to the goal-centredness of the Western culture is to miss the point. Only in increased openness and spontaneity will grace be given. In letting go of the fruits of our labours, of our need to control, or even to know, we can find stillness in the present.

But later Walsche makes his meaning clear: "Most people think that 'going home' means returning to God. But you cannot return to God, because you never left God, *and your soul knows this...* You are not going to get back Home. You never left Home" (*ibid.*, 27, 186). Or as Matthew Fox put it: "The divine home. God is here. It is we who have gone out for a walk."

He says that in meditation "We learn to be at home in the dark as well as in the light; in sadness as well as in joy; in success, and in the poverty of failure."

Suzanne talks of "a sense of home... during deep meditation in that timeless place of having no where to get; to just be in that eternal present state of oneness." Silence is after all where those in closest relationship are at home – there is no need for speech.

That spiritual sense of home can be found anywhere. Pausing during the day wherever we are: centring, collecting ourselves, taking a step back from the preoccupation, the mood of the moment, breathing into a deeper reality. In summer I sometimes walk in the early morning in the local park, feeling the soft earth underfoot, the grass between my bare toes. One morning I came across an Asian woman sitting on a bench, practising yogic alternate nostril breathing. Further on, I discovered an Asian man – her husband? – practising the fire breath. Unselfconscious, lost in the breath. Heartened by their absorption, I decided to join them, so I, too, sat alone on a bench and breathed, first one way and then the other.

A Quaker Meeting for Worship held at Speakers Corner in Hyde Park, London, is an extraordinary experience. In the midst of the hubbub of soap box preaching, shouting and heckling, a small circle of silent worshippers forms, and gradually there develops a sense of holding a still centre. At vigils held at nuclear power bases, or outside embassies, the same sense prevails. Not cutting itself off from all that surrounds it, but absorbing external noises into a worshipful presence. Pausing in stillness in a noisy restaurant before a meal can also provide a strong sense of centre and presence. There is something palpable.

Ishwari is an American *swamini*. She took *sannyasi diksha* (initiation as a wandering mendicant and ascetic) a couple of years ago, and practises obedience to her Swami. "I guess I could say a lot about home since Swamiji has moved me around so much in the last several years. I've learned that home is inside of you and that each physical place you call 'home' has its own lessons to teach, its own gifts and its own sorrows. Every new place is like entering a new dimension."

A young lawyer living in England says: "Home is not a physical place, but somewhere I'm looking for – I know it's somewhere here [touching his solar plexus]. It will be my spiritual homecoming. It's wherever I have that encounter (with God)."

Some years ago I was part of a workshop that asked us to draw our idea of God – as it used to be, as it was then, and as we thought it might be in the future.

For the first part I drew my childhood view of an old man with a white beard on a cloud.

For the second I drew a beautiful landscape with sun and moon, and plants and life and human beings and animals.

For the future, I drew O.

III. Home

When I began to write this book, I had no clear sense of what home was for me, but, in talking to others, in the writing, a clearer picture has emerged. As for others, it has been different things at different times of my life.

A few weeks ago my children and I went through the family photos – photos I had not looked at since the break-up of my marriage twenty years ago. It was striking how we agreed on the seminal images: the pictures that spoke of the moment in a way that we all recognised: a fifth birthday party; my father's look of love as he put his arm round my daughter in her high chair; my ex-husband, pencil in mouth, very much the young exec. Snapshots not of houses but of our family life.

There are other, virtual, snapshots of my life: a warm kitchen with myself as a teenager, doing my homework at the table, or listening to the radio; later, in the arms of a man I loved, sleepily breastfeeding a child in the middle of the night. Scenes of the family later – laughing, playing cards, and outside, in the sun; and with people who know me well, who accept me as I am. In wide flat landscapes, big skies, alone with the birds. Singing. The exhilaration of feeling in the right place. The joy of working with slum children in India:

> I had done some work with homeless people in London, and my feeling as I got off the bone-shaker bus at the first slum, was the same. As I joined the young local teacher in wandering through the black plastic "growing frame" tents calling, "School, school, *jaldi, jaldi*", I felt a swelling of my heart, a lump in my throat and the conviction that these were "my" people (Kavanagh, 2004: 155-6).

In rural South Africa:

> Cynthia …is as passionate about the programme as I am; we are both at home hiking out to the villages, umbrellas up against the sun or the rain, working with local women in their homes to enable them to start up businesses.

Or simply glorying in our natural habitat:

> I love the desert: in such landscapes my soul expands... Sometimes during the hours of driving I persuaded the others to go ahead for a few miles and brew up while I walked on. Outside I jumped up and down, danced for joy. I wanted to

spend hours, days just walking in the wilderness into the immeasurable distance. Because I could see the van, a dot on the horizon, I sometimes turned and walked backwards to give myself the illusion of solitude. I wanted to be alone (Kavanagh, 2004: 168).

Such snapshots, whether tangible or virtual, are personal: each will be able to call up her own. But, however they come, we can probably all recognise the moments of stillness, of a wider perspective, of access to a deeper reality. Unexpected, spontaneous moments of joy, peace or contentment. Moments of grace.

Home is not always where I am, for I am not always at home to myself. But, increasingly, I am. In that still, centred place of contentment. When I am open to the spirit in all creation. When I have left guilt and fear behind and am in true relation with myself and with all about me. At peace.

In the end, the answer to the question we started with – "Where do you live?" – is "here, anywhere, where I am now".

Your true home is in the here and the now. It is not limited by time, space, nationality, or race. Your true home is not an abstract idea. It is something you can touch and live in every moment. With mindfulness and concentration, the energies of the Buddha, you can find your true home in the full relaxation of your mind and body in the present moment. No one can take it away from you. Other people can occupy your country, they can even put you in prison, but they cannot take away your true home and your freedom (Thich Nhat Hanh, "Returning Home", *Shambhala*, March 2006).

That combination of home and freedom is key. Finding home brings freedom. For home, as we know it, is not merely a static state, found once and for all. A material home is a place of security from which to go out into the world and express our fullness, and it may take many forms. In the spiritual dimension, there is a balance to be found between rootedness and the spiritual quest. Sustainability is akin to justice, not just for future generations, but in the sense of balance, harmony, equilibrium: within society, within the species, within the cosmos, within the self. Einstein said that the most important question is: "Is the universe a friendly place?" Maybe we could add to that, "Are we?"

The more we find home in ourselves, the more we will be able to express it in our relationships with others, and the less we will need it expressed in our material surroundings. The more we express that self in the world and in the work we do, the less we will need to compensate for feelings of inadequacy or alienation by larger, more separate, more fashionable or even more beautiful houses, furniture and artefacts. The more we trust in our real selves, the more love and the less fear we will feel. A physical home will not need to be an escape, nor a refuge buttressed against a hostile world, but a shelter merely from the cold and wet, and an open-hearted place of true hospitality.

The more we are at home in ourselves, the less we will feel the need to scapegoat others, to project on to stigmatised groups of people our own fear of difference, our own lack of belonging. We will not need to shore up the borders of our soul, our community or our country against the "other", because fear and borders will dissolve in loving acceptance of the oneness expressed in such rich and astonishing diversity.

When we are truly at home, we will understand our place alongside fellow creatures on this planet, the deep mutuality of all life-forms, and the need to heal what we have wounded. We will better understand what we are continually given by other living beings, and will have a wish to give something back; at the very least to bring to consciousness the beauty and preciousness of creation. We will recognise with humility our place as tiny points in space and time in the universe, and realise how much there is that we do not understand.

Home is not static. Home is the balance between security and freedom; of belonging and longing. Home is both an end and a beginning.

Follow-up questions

Chapter 1: Introduction
What does the word "home" mean to you?
Does where you live feel like home?
Why?/Why not?

Chapter 2: Bricks and mortar
What are the necessary physical attributes of a home?
How important is the physical security of where you live?
How important is it to own your house/flat?

Chapter 3: Homeless
Have you ever been homeless, or worried that you might be?
What do you do when asked for money by a homeless person?
    How do you feel?

Chapter 4: On the move
Have you ever lived in a mobile home? If so, how did it feel?
Are you attracted by a nomadic life?
Why?/Why not?

Chapter 5: Home is where the heart is
Did where you live as a child feel like home?
Why?/Why not?
How did it feel when you left home?
Have you consciously created a home? How?
Does a home need more than one person?

Chapter 6: Community
Do you feel part of a community?
Why?/Why not?
Who is included/excluded from your local community?

What first step could you make to create an ideal community?

Chapter 7: Not at home
When is a home not a home?
Have you ever felt homesick?

Chapter 8: Borders and belonging
What are your roots?
How important is your nationality?
What makes up your national identity?

Chapter 9: Displacement
Have you ever felt an outsider?
Have you ever had to leave your country?
How can your country be made a more welcoming place for
   refugees?

Chapter 10: Our sacred home
Do you relate to the life-force in other beings?
Do you feel responsible for the way we treat the planet?
Is there anything you can do about it?

Chapter 11: Coming home
Is home a physical place?
When do you feel at home in yourself?
Do you relate to something higher than yourself?
Has your concept of home been changed by reading this book?

Further Reading

Alexander, Christopher, *The Timeless Way of Building*. New York: Oxford University Press, 1979

Alexander, Christopher, et al., *A Pattern Language*. New York: Oxford University Press, 1977

Berry, Thomas, *Evening Thoughts*. San Francisco: Sierra Club, 2006

Best, Marigold, & Hussey, Pamela, *Women Making a Difference*. London: SPCK, 2001

Buber, Martin, *I and Thou*. London: Continuum, reprint 2007

Capra, Fritjof, Steindl-Rast, David, with Matus, Thomas, *Belonging to the Universe*. London: Penguin, 1992

Chapman, Serle L., *We, The People of Earth and Elders*, Vol II. Missoula, Montana: Mountain Press, 2001

De Botton, Alain, *The Architecture of Happiness*. London: Penguin, 2007

Ephraums, Eddie, *The Big Issue Book of Home*. London: The *Big Issue* and Hodder & Stoughton, 2000

Fox, Matthew, *Original Blessing*. Santa Fe: Bear & Co, 1983

Frazier, Ian, *On the Rez*. NY: Farrar, Straus & Giroux, 2000

Hoffman, Eva, *Lost in Translation*. London: Vintage, 1991

Jones, Tobias, *Utopian Dreams*. London: Faber & Faber, 2007

Katz, Michael, Marsh, William P., Thompson, Gail Gordon, *Earth's Answer*. New York: Harper & Row, 1977

King, Russell (ed.), *The History of Human Migration*. London: Marshall Editions, 2007

Kumar, Satish, "Schumacher lecture", 30 October 2004

Kurlansky, Mark, *The Basque History of the World*. London: Vintage, 2000.

Mayhew, Henry, *London Labour and the London Poor*. Selected by Victor Neuburg, Penguin, 1985

Moorehead, Caroline, *Human Cargo*. Vintage, 2006

Nouwen, Henri, *Reaching Out*. New York: Doubleday, 1975

O'Donohue, John, *Anam Cara*. London: Bantam, 1999

Pan, Lynn, *Sons of the Yellow Emperor*. London: Mandarin, 1996

Palmer, Guy, Kenway, Peter and Wilcox, Steve, *Housing and Neighbourhoods Monitor*. York: Joseph Rowntree Foundation, 2006

Sacks, Jonathan, *To heal a Fractured World*. London: Continuum, 2005

Smolan, Rick and Erwitt, Jennifer. *UK At Home: A close-up look at how we live*. London: Duncan Baird, 2008

The Who Cares? Trust, *The Journey Home*. 2006

Thoreau, Henry David, *Walden, or Life in the Woods*. New York: Dover, 1995

Tolstoy, Leo, trans. Jane Kentish, "What is religion and of what does it consist?" in *A Confession and other religious writings*. London: Penguin, 1987

Tunstall, Rebecca, "Estate Secrets: How twenty council estates survived the twentieth century", unpublished thesis.

Vardey, Lucinda (ed.), *God in All Worlds*. New York: Vintage, 1995

Walker, Graham, *Unsettled: In a Hole, climbed a mountain, the life of a Big Issue man*. Naked Guides, 2007

Walsche, Neale Donald, *Home with God*. London: Hodder & Stoughton, 2006

BOOKS

O is a symbol of the world, of oneness and unity. In different cultures it also means the "eye," symbolizing knowledge and insight. We aim to publish books that are accessible, constructive and that challenge accepted opinion, both that of academia and the "moral majority."

Our books are available in all good English language bookstores worldwide. If you don't see the book on the shelves ask the bookstore to order it for you, quoting the ISBN number and title. Alternatively you can order online (all major online retail sites carry our titles) or contact the distributor in the relevant country, listed on the copyright page.

See our website www.o-books.net for a full list of over 500 titles, growing by 100 a year.

And tune in to myspiritradio.com for our book review radio show, hosted by June-Elleni Laine, where you can listen to the authors discussing their books.

MySpiritRadio